A

FEW NOTES ON SHAKESPEARE.

AMS PRESS
NEW YORK

A FEW NOTES

ON

SHAKESPEARE;

WITH

OCCASIONAL REMARKS ON THE EMENDATIONS OF THE
MANUSCRIPT-CORRECTOR IN MR. COLLIER'S
COPY OF THE FOLIO 1632.

BY

THE REV. ALEXANDER DYCE.

LONDON:
JOHN RUSSELL SMITH, 36 SOHO SQUARE.

MDCCCLIII.

Reprinted from a copy in the collection of the
Brooklyn Public Library

Reprinted from the edition of 1853, London
First AMS EDITION published 1971
Manufactured in the United States of America

International Standard Book Number: 0-404-02228-6

Library of Congress Catalog Number: 71-164813

AMS PRESS INC.
NEW YORK, N.Y. 10003

PREFACE.

In the course of the following remarks I have endeavoured to shew that sundry of the recently-published *Emendations* by the Manuscript-corrector of the folio 1632 are altogether erroneous; and I might have noticed a variety of others by that mysterious personage, which, I feel assured, are such as cannot stand the test of criticism. But the reader must not therefore suppose that I consider Mr. Collier's volume as useless to the future editors of Shakespeare: my opinion is, that while it abounds with alterations ignorant, tasteless, and wanton, it also occasionally presents corrections which require no authority to recommend them, because common sense declares them to be right.

Since these sheets were printed off, I have found that the quotation from Cotgrave at p. 71 was long ago adduced by Mr. Singer in his edition of Shakespeare; and that the emendation given as my own at p. 36 had previously occurred to the same gentleman.

A. D.

CONTENTS.

	PAGE
THE TEMPEST	9
THE TWO GENTLEMEN OF VERONA	17
THE MERRY WIVES OF WINDSOR	18
MEASURE FOR MEASURE	24
THE COMEDY OF ERRORS	28
MUCH ADO ABOUT NOTHING	37
LOVE'S LABOUR'S LOST	48
A MIDSUMMER-NIGHT'S DREAM	61
THE MERCHANT OF VENICE	64
AS YOU LIKE IT	68
THE TAMING OF THE SHREW	70
ALL'S WELL THAT ENDS WELL	72
TWELFTH NIGHT	75
THE WINTER'S TALE	79
KING JOHN	83
RICHARD II.	92
FIRST PART OF HENRY IV.	93
SECOND PART OF HENRY IV.	97
SECOND PART OF HENRY VI.	99
THIRD PART OF HENRY VI.	101
RICHARD III.	103
HENRY VIII.	105

CONTENTS.

	PAGE
TROILUS AND CRESSIDA	107
ROMEO AND JULIET	109
JULIUS CÆSAR	116
MACBETH	118
HAMLET	134
KING LEAR	146
OTHELLO	147
ANTONY AND CLEOPATRA	150
CYMBELINE	155

A FEW NOTES,

ETC.

THE TEMPEST.

Act i. sc. 2.

" The sky, it seems, would pour down stinking pitch,
But that the sea, mounting to the welkin's *cheek*,
Dashes the fire out."

" The manuscript corrector of the folio, 1632, has substituted *heat* for 'cheek,' which is not an unlikely corruption by a person writing only by the ear." Collier's *Notes and Emendations, &c.* p. 2. " On the whole, *heat* in this place seems to be one of those alterations, which, though supported by some probability, it might be inexpedient to insert in the text." *Id.* p. 503.

I must be allowed to protest against the Manuscript-corrector's "*heat*," as *not* supported by *any* probability: in fact, it is an alteration equally tasteless and absurd.

Act i. sc. 2.
" Lend thy hand,
And pluck my magic garment from me.—So;
[*Lays down his mantle.*
Lie there my art.*"

Here Steevens observes (from Fuller), that "Lord Burleigh, when he put off his gown at night, used to say, *Lie there, Lord Treasurer.*"—So in *A Pleasant Commodie called Looke about you,* which was printed in 1600 (and therefore preceded *The Tempest*), Skinke puts off his hermit's robes with a similar expression;

> "*Rob.* Adew, good father.—Holla there, my horse!
> [*Exit.*
> *Skin.* Vp-spur the kicking jade, while I make speede
> To conjure Skinke out of his hermits weede.
> *Lye there religion.*"
> Sig. A 2.

and in Chettle's *Tragedy of Hoffman*, 1631 (which was also an earlier play than *The Tempest**), Lorrique, throwing off the disguise of a French doctor, says;

> "*Doctor lie there.* Lorrique, like thyselfe appeare."
> Sig. G.

I may add, that in Shadwell's *Virtuoso,* Sir Samuel Harty lays aside his female dress with the words, " So, *tyrewoman, lie thou there.*" Act iv. p. 388, *Works,* ed. 1720.

Act i. sc. 2.
" With *hair up-staring.*"

Many readers of Shakespeare are perhaps not aware how common this expression was formerly. It not only found a place in the most serious poetry, as here, and in Chapman's *Hero and Leander* (Marlowe's *Works,* iii. 91. ed. Dyce), but belonged to the phraseology of daily life:

---

* See Henslowe's *Diary*, p. 229, ed. Shak. Soc.

"*Les cheveux luy dressent.* His *haire stares,* or stands annend." Cotgrave's Dict. sub *Dresser;* and compare Florio's *Dict.* sub *Arricciare.*

Act i. sc. 2.
"*Foot it featly* here and there."

This expression, which is now so familiar to us from Ariel's song, was certainly an unusual one in the days of Shakespeare, who probably caught it from a line in Lodge's *Glaucus and Scilla,* 1589,—

"*Footing it featlie* on the grassie ground."
Sig. A 2.

Act i. sc. 2.
" my prime request,
Which I do last pronounce, is, O you wonder!
If you be *maid* or no?
    Mira.   No wonder, sir;
But, certainly a *maid.*"

In a note on this passage, in his ed. of *Shakespeare,* Mr. Collier observes; "Ferdinand has at first supposed Miranda a goddess, and now inquires if she be really a mortal; not a celestial being, but a maiden. 'Maid' is used in its general sense. *Miranda's answer is to be taken in the same sense as Ferdinand's question.*"

I differ entirely from Mr. Collier about the meaning of Miranda's answer. She plays on the word *maid:*—
"But, certainly *a maid,*" *i. e.* a virgin.

Act iii. sc. 1.

"But these sweet thoughts do even refresh my labours;
Most *busy-less* when I do it."

The first folio has,

"Most *busy lest*, when I do it;"

the second folio,

"Most *busy, least* when I do it."

The reading "*busy-less*" is Theobald's. According to Mr. Collier (*Notes and Emendations*, &c. p. 11), the controversy about this passage "seems set at rest by the manuscript correction in the folio 1632;" which is,—

"'Most busy—*blest*, when I do it.'

That is to say, he deems himself *blest* even by heavy toils, when they are made light by the thoughts of Miranda; he was 'most busy,' but still *blest*, when so employed. It is right to add that this emendation is, like a few others, upon an erasure, as if something had been written there before: perhaps the page had been blotted."

Now, I decidedly think—that the Manuscript-corrector's emendation is forced and awkward in the very extreme;—that Mr. Collier is as unsuccessful in defending it, as he was when in his edition of *Shakespeare* he defended the old misprint, "Most *busy, least;*"—and that the conjecture of Theobald, "*busy-less*," is far more likely to be the true reading than the Manuscript-corrector's scarcely intelligible alteration, which (as is plain from what is stated about the erasure) was not his first attempt to set the passage right.

Act iv. sc. 1.

> "*Pro.* If I have too austerely punish'd you,
> Your compensation makes amends; for I
> Have given you here a *thread* of mine own life
> Or that for which I live."

Mr. Collier observes (*Notes and Emendations*, &c. p. 12); "The text has been much disputed, and for 'third' of the old printed copy, the corrector of the folio, 1632, has written *thrid* (*i.e.* thread) in the margin. This fact may possibly be decisive of the question."

Mr. Collier is hardly justified in saying that "the text has been *much* disputed." "Thread" has been adopted by all the recent editors, except Mr. Collier himself, who strenuously supported what he is now willing to reject on the authority of the Manuscript-corrector.

In case any future editor should still be inclined to make Prospero term Miranda "a *third* of his life," it may be well to remark here,—that in the language of poetry, from the earliest times, a beloved object has always been spoken of, not as the *third*, but as the HALF of another's life or soul: (so Meleager, ἀμισύ μευ ψυχῆς; and Horace, "animæ dimidium meæ").

Act iv. sc. 1.

> "And, like this insubstantial pageant faded,
> Leave not a *rack* behind."

So this famous passage stands in all editions old and new. But I believe that Malone's objection to the reading, "*a rack*," is unanswerable. "No instance," he observes, "has yet been produced where *rack* is used to signify *a single small fleeting cloud;*" in other words,—though our early writers very frequently make mention of "*the* rack," they never say "*a* rack." Malone adds, "I incline to think that *rack* is a mis-spelling for *wrack, i.e.* wreck;" and I now am thoroughly convinced that such is the case. In authors of the age of Elizabeth and James I have repeatedly met with *rack* put for *wrack;* and in all the early editions of Milton's *Paradise Lost* which I possess,— viz. the first, 1667, the second, 1674, the third, 1678, the fourth, 1688, and the eighth, 1707,—I find,—

" Now dreadful deeds
Might have ensued, nor only Paradise
In this commotion, but the starry cope
Of Heaven perhaps, or all the elements
At least had gone to *rack* [i. e. *wrack*=wreck]," &c.
B. iv. 990.
" A world devote to universal *rack* [i. e. *wrack*=wreck]."
B. xi. 821.

Act iv. sc. 1.
" Come, hang them on this *line.*"

" To the old stage-direction, *Enter Ariel, loaden with glistering apparel,* the manuscript corrector of the folio, 1632, has added the explanatory words, *Hang it on the line;* but whether we are to understand a *line tree* (as has been suggested by Mr. Hunter, in his learned Essay on the Tempest, 8vo. 1839), or a mere rope, is not stated." Collier's *Notes and Emendations,* &c. p. 13.

With all my respect for Mr. Hunter's learned labours, I must confess that I think him entirely wrong in the matter of the "*line.*"

If no other objections could be urged against Mr. Hunter's acceptation of the word *line,* we surely have a decisive one in the joke of Stephano, " Now, jerkin, you are like to lose your hair,"—a joke to which it is impossible to attach any meaning, unless we suppose that the *line* was a *hair-line*. Mr. Knight observes; "In a woodcut of twelve distinct figures of trades and callings of the time of James I. (see Smith's 'Cries of London,' p. 15), and of which there is a copy in the British Museum, we have the cry of ' *Buy a hair-line!*' " And in Lyly's *Midas*, a barber's apprentice facetiously says, "All my mistres' lynes that she dryes her cloathes on, are made only of Mustachio stuffe [*i. e.* of the cuttings of moustachios]." Sig. G 2, ed. 1592.

Act iv. sc. 1.

" *Cal.* The dropsy drown this fool! what do you mean,
To doat thus on such luggage ? *Let's alone,*
And do the murder first."

So the old copies. Mr. Knight follows them, quoting Steevens's preposterous suggestion that " '*Let's alone*' may mean—' Let you and I only go to commit the murder, leaving Trinculo, who is so solicitous about the *trash* of dress, behind us.' "—Mr. Collier prints (with a novel abbreviation) " *Let* 't *alone.*"—Malone alters " *Let's alone*" to " *Let* it *alone,*"—because, he says, " Caliban has used the expression before,"—the very reason (as will be evident to any one who carefully compares the two passages) why it should not be repeated here.

Has none of the commentators, then, been led by the words, " And do the murder first," to the lection obviously required in what immediately precedes ? Yes: Theobald's sagacity did not forsake him here; but his certain emendation is now only to be found among the rubbish of the *Variorum Shakespeare*, in a very foolish note by Malone, which concludes with, " Mr. Theobald reads —' Let's along' "!

Act v. sc. 1.

" *The entrance of the Cell opens, and discovers* FERDINAND *and* MIRANDA *playing at chess.*"

There may have been something like this in the novel or tale which furnished Shakespeare with the materials for *The Tempest;* but if that was not the case, and if *The Tempest* was first produced shortly before the year 1611, it is not improbable that the idea of " discovering" Ferdinand and Miranda engaged at chess was suggested to Shakespeare by a similar " discovery" in Barnaby Barnes's *Divils Charter*, printed in 1607 (" *As it was plaide before the King's Maiestie, vpon Candlemasse night last, by his Maiesties Seruants. But more exactly reuewed, corrected, and augmented since by the Author for the more pleasure and profit of the Reader*").

In that tragedy, Cæsar Borgia, after taking Katherine prisoner and making her believe that he had put to death her two sons, says,—

" Come hither, Katherine, wonder of thy sex,
The grace of all Italian womanhood.
Cæsar shall neuer prooue dishonourable:
Behold thy children liuing in my tent.
He discoureth his Tent where her two sonnes were at Cardes."

Sig. I.

THE TWO GENTLEMEN OF VERONA.

Act i. sc. 1.

"*Speed.* Twenty to one, then, he is *shipp'd* already,
And I have play'd the *sheep* in losing him."

To the examples given by the editors of *ship* used for *sheep*, add the following one; " A hood shall flap up and downe heere, and this *ship*-skin cap shall be put off." Dekker's *Satiromastix*, 1602, sig. F 3.

Act i. sc. 1.

" a laced mutton."

In this very common cant expression for a courtesan, the meaning of *laced* has (like many other things equally unimportant) been a good deal disputed. Perhaps the *mutton* was called *laced* with a quibble—courtesans being notoriously fond of finery, and also frequently subjected to the whip : Du Bartas tells us that St. Louis put down the stews,

" *Lacing with lashes* their unpitied skin
Whom lust or lucre had bestowed therein."
Works, by Sylvester,—*St. Louis the King*,
p. 539, ed. 1641.

But in the present passage is " *laced mutton*" to be regarded as synonymous with *courtesan?* I doubt it. When Speed applies that term to Julia, he probably uses it in the much less offensive sense of—*a richly-attired piece of woman's flesh*.

c

THE MERRY WIVES OF WINDSOR.

Act i. sc. 3.

" Let me see thee *froth*, and lime."

" The first," says Steevens, " was done by putting soap into the bottom of the tankard when they drew the beer; the other, by mixing *lime* with the sack (*i. e.* sherry) to make it sparkle in the glass."

But I question if there be any allusion in this passage to frothing beer *by means of soap*. Compare Greene's *Quip for an Vpstart Courtier;* " You, *Tom Tapster*, that tap your small cans of beere to the poore, and yet *fill them halfe full of froth*," &c. Sig. F 2, ed. 1620.

Act i. sc. 3.

" she discourses, she *carves*, she gives the leer of invitation."

Mr. Collier (*Notes and Emendations*, &c. p. 30) writes thus. "A misprint in the old editions of ' carves' for *craves*, has occasioned some difficulty in the passage where Falstaff, speaking of the expected result of his enterprise against Mrs. Ford, observes, as the words have been invariably given, ' I spy entertainment in her; she discourses, she carves, she gives the leer of invitation.' A note in the margin of the corrected folio, 1632, shews that we ought to read ' she *craves*, she gives the leer of invitation.' There seems no sufficient reason for supposing that ' carves' ought to be taken in the figurative sense of *wooes;* and although ladies might now and then ' carve' to guests, in the literal meaning of the word (as in the passage quoted by Boswell from Webster's 'Vittoria Corombona,' Shakesp. by Malone, viii. 38), yet carving was undoubtedly an accomplishment peculiarly belonging to men. Falstaff evidently, from the context, intends to say that Mrs. Ford has a *craving* for him, and therefore gave 'the leer of invitation.' The misprint was a very easy one, occasioned merely by the transposition of a letter, and any forced construction is needless."

I read with something more than surprise this elaborate defence of "*craves*,"—an alteration which (whether made by the Manuscript-corrector *suo periculo*, or derived by him from the prompter's-book) originated in sheer ignorance of the word *carve* having been occasionally employed, at an earlier period, in a sense altogether different from that of *cutting up meat*. And surely, if Mr. Collier had been acquainted with Mr. Hunter's remarks on that peculiar use of the word, he would at once have acknowledged that here the Manuscript-corrector is egregiously mistaken.

Mr. Hunter (*New Illustr. of Shakespeare*, i. 215), comparing the present passage with that in *Love's Labour's lost*, act v. sc. 2,—

" He can *carve* too and lisp : why, this is he
That kiss'd away his hand in courtesy,"—

observes; "The commentators have no other idea of the word *carve*, than that it denotes the particular action of carving at table. But it is a quite different word. It occurs in a very rare poetic tract, entitled *A Prophecie of Cadwallader, last King of the Brittaines,* by William Herbert, 4to. 1604, which opens with a description of Fortune, and of some who had sought to gain her favour :

' Then did this Queen her wandering coach ascend,
  Whose wheels were more inconstant than the wind :
A mighty troop this empress did attend ;
  There might you Caius Marius *carving* find,
  And martial Sylla courting Venus kind.' "

To the lines adduced by Mr. Hunter, I have to add the following passages.

" Her amorous glances are her accusers ; her very lookes write sonnets in thy commendations ; she *carues* thee at boord, and cannot sleepe for dreaming on thee in bedde." Day's *Ile of Gulls*, 1606, sig. D.

" And, if thy rival be in presence too,
  Seem not to mark, but do as others do ;
  Salute him friendly, give him gentle words,
  Return all courtesies that he affords ;
  Drink to him, *carve* him, give him compliment ;
  This shall thy mistress more than thee torment."
        Beaumont's *Remedy of Love*,*—B. and Fletcher's
              Works, xi. 483, ed. Dyce.

" Desire to eat with her, *carve* her, drink to her, and still among intermingle your petition of grace and acceptance into her favour." Fletcher and Shakespeare's *Two Noble Kinsmen*,—B. and Fletcher's *Works*, xi. 414, ed. Dyce (where Seward, thinking that *the cutting up of meat* was in question, silently printed " carve for *her*").

---

* Beaumont's *Remedy of Love* is a very free imitation of Ovid's *Remedia Amoris ;* and (as far as I can discover) the only part of the original which answers to the present passage is—

" Hunc quoque, quo quondam nimium rivale dolebas,
  Vellem desineres hostis habere loco.
At certe, quamvis odio remanente, *saluta*."
                              v. 791.

Carving, says Mr. Hunter, "would seem to mean some form of action which indicated the desire that the person to whom it was addressed should be attentive and propitious." Whatever was its exact nature, it would appear, from the three passages last cited, to have been a sort of salutation which was practised more especially at table.*

To return, for a moment, to the Manuscript-corrector's emendation. Does Mr. Collier see nothing absurd in "Mrs. Ford *craving* (*i. e.* having a craving for) *Falstaff?*"—(she *might* have had a craving for a Windsor pear.) Is he sensible of no impropriety in "*craving*" (a word which expresses not an *action,* but a *feeling*) being interposed between "she *discourses*" and "she *gives the leer of invitation?*"

Act ii. sc. 1.
" Will you go, *An-heires?*"

" Warburton suggested '*heris,* the old Scotch word for master;' Steevens, *hearts;* Malone, *hear us;* Boaden, *cava-*

* Mr. Halliwell, in his *Dict. of Arch. and Prov. Words,* has ; " CARVE. To woo. Mr. Hunter, Illustrations, i. 215, has the merit of pointing out the peculiar use of this word, although he has not discovered its meaning, which is clearly ascertained from the use of the substantive *carver* in Lilly's Mother Bombie, ' neither father nor mother, kith nor kinne, shall bee her *carver* in a husband ; shee will fall too where shee likes best.' "—I cannot agree with Mr. Halliwell in thinking that the meaning of *carve* is ascertained by this passage from *Mother Bombie :* in fact, Lilly there uses " *carver*" in its common acceptation, as is manifest from the conclusion of the passage,—" shee will *fall to* where shee likes best." Compare *Don Quixote ;* " ' Why, an't please you,' quoth Sancho, ' Teresa bids me make sure work with your worship, and that we may have less talking and more doing; *that a man must not be his own carver ;* that he who cuts does not shuffle,' " &c. Vol. iii. 200, ed. Edin. 1822. (Motteux's trans.)

liers, &c. The manuscript corrector of the folio, 1632, merely changes one letter, and omits two, and leaves the passage, ' Will you go *on, here?*' * * * It is singular that nobody seems ever to have conjectured that *on here* might be concealed under 'An-heires.'" Collier's *Notes and Emendations*, &c. p. 33.

To me it appears altogether unlikely that two such common words as "*on here*" should have been mistaken, either by copyist or compositor, for "An-heires:" and I apprehend that, when the Manuscript-corrector altered the *vox nihili* by "*merely* changing one letter and omitting two," he at the same time was far from feeling confident that "*on here*" was "concealed under *An-heires*."

There is a passage in act ii. sc. 3 of Fletcher's *Beggars' Bush*, as exhibited in the folio, 1647, which, unless I am much deceived, enables us to determine positively what word ought to take the place of "An-heires" in the text of the great dramatist. For my own part at least,—since I find in that folio, p. 80,

" Nay, Sir, *mine heire* Van-dunck
Is a true Statesman,"—

I can no longer doubt that "*An*-heires" is a misprint for "*Min*-heires," and that Hanmer (whose emendation Mr. Collier does not even notice) restored the genuine reading, when he altered " Will you go, *An-heires?*" to " Will you go, *Mynheers?*"

We have no reason to suppose that the word *Mynheer* (which, as we have just seen, is used by Fletcher) was less known in England when Shakespeare wrote *The Merry Wives of Windsor* than it is at present (perhaps, indeed, by means of the soldiers who returned from the wars in the

Netherlands, it was formerly better known than now); nor is there any reason why it should not have been in the Host's vocabulary as well as *bully-rook*.*

* I may just observe that " Bully-*rock*" (which is only another form of the word) occurs over and over again in Shadwell's *Sullen Lovers:* see his *Works*, vol. i. pp. 26, 37, 45, 46, 62, 69, 74, 83, 84, 101, 102, 108.

MEASURE FOR MEASURE.

Act i. sc. 2.

"*Bawd.* What's to do here, *Thomas* Tapster?"

"Why," says Douce, "does she call the clown by this name, when it appears from his own showing that his name was *Pompey*? Perhaps she is only quoting some old saying or ballad."

Because *Thomas* or *Tom* was the name commonly applied to a *Tapster;* for the sake of the alliteration, it would seem. See the passage cited from Greene, at p. 18.

Act ii. sc. 2.

"How would you be,
If he, which is the *top* of judgment, should
But judge you as you are?"

"We meet," says Mr. Collier, "with a bold and striking emendation in one of Isabella's noble appeals to Angelo . . . . . The amended folio, 1632, has it,—

'How would you be,
If he, which is the *God* of judgment, should
But judge you as you are?'

This is not to be considered at all in the light of a profane use of the name of the Creator, as in oaths and exclamations; and while *top* may easily have been misheard by the scribe for 'God,' the latter word, though the meaning is of course the same, adds to the power and grandeur of the passage." *Notes and Emendations,* &c. p. 45.

What Mr. Collier calls "a bold and striking emendation," deserves rather to be characterised as rash and wanton in the extreme.

That very expression, which did not suit the taste of the Manuscript-corrector, occurs in another mighty poet,— one whose fame is as imperishable as Shakespeare's. In the sixth Canto of the *Purgatorio*, Dante, having met with certain spirits who were anxious to obtain the prayers of the living, thus addresses his conductor;

> " E' par che tu mi nieghi,
> O luce mia, espresso in alcun testo,
> Che decreto del Cielo orazion pieghi:
> E queste genti pregan pur di questo.
> Sarebbe dunque loro speme vana?
> O non m' è il detto tuo ben manifesto?"

Virgil replies;

> " La mia scrittura è piana,
> E la speranza di costor non falla,
> Se ben si guarda con la mente sana;
> Chè *cima di giudicio* non s' avvalla,
> Perchè foco d' amor compia in un punto
> Ciò che dee soddisfar chi qui s' astalla," &c.
>
> v. 28, sqq.

Act ii. sc. 2.

" Not with fond *shekels* of the tested gold," &c.

" It is spelt *sickles* in the old copies, but the true word may be *circles;* and the manuscript corrector of the folio, 1632, has altered 'sickles' to *sirkles*, paying no other attention to the spelling of the word. Nevertheless 'shekels' may be right, and it is used, exactly with the same spelling, by Lodge in his 'Catharos,' 1591, sign. c, where we read,

' Here in Athens the father hath suffred his sonne to bee hanged for forty *sickles*, and hee worth four hundred talents.'" *Notes and Emendations*, &c. p. 45.

After the quotation from Lodge, Mr. Collier might have been sure that the Manuscript-corrector's alteration was quite wrong. Compare also Peele's *David and Bethsabe;*

" That so I might have given thee for thy pains
Ten silver *shekels* [old ed. " sickles"] and a golden waist."
Works, ii. 63, ed. Dyce, 1829.

" *Circles of gold*," I conceive, could only mean *crowns* (*diadems*) *of gold*. (In *Macbeth*, act i. sc. 5, we have " the golden round," *i. e.* diadem.)

Act iii. sc. 1.
" Servile to all the *skyey* influences."

Our lexicographers adduce no other example of "*skyey*" except the present. Perhaps Shakespeare found it in a writer, from whom (as will afterwards be shewn) he borrowed a remarkable expression for *Macbeth;*

" So on I hasted at my jades behest,
As whilom Phaeton in his *skyey* carte," &c.
A Fig for Fortune, 1596, by Anthony Copley, p. 20.

Act iii. sc. 1.
" her combinate husband."

The late W. S. Rose, after giving some instances of the " close and whimsical relation there often is between English and Italian idiom," concludes with this remark. " Thus every Italian scholar understands ' her *combinate husband*' to mean her husband elect; and at this hour there is nothing more commonly in an Italian's mouth than ' Se si puo *combinarla*' (if we can bring it to bear), when speaking with reference to any future arrangement." Note on his translation of *Orlando Furioso*, vol. iv. 47.

THE COMEDY OF ERRORS.

Act ii. sc. 1.

" *Ant. S.* You would all this time have proved, there is no time for all things.

" *Dro. S.* Marry, and did, sir; namely *in no* time to recover hair lost by nature."

So the first folio erroneously reads. Malone printed " namely, *e'en* no time" (which sounds oddly enough); and Mr. Collier adopts it, without mentioning that it is a modern reading,—a very unusual oversight in him.

The second folio gives what is evidently right,— " namely, no time to recover hair lost by nature."

Act iii. sc. 1.

" Maud, Bridget, Marian, Cicely, Gillian, *Gin*."

In this line, though it rhymes with one ending in " let us *in*," the modern editors (with the exception of Mr. Collier, who retains the above spelling) print " Jen'."

The name should be spelt "Jin" (a contraction of *Jinny;* see Cotgrave's *Dict.* in *Jannette*).

Act iii. sc. 1.

" *Luce.* Have at you with another; that's,— *When? can you tell?*"

This proverbial question occurs in Day's *Law-Trickes*, 1608;

" Still good in law ; ile fetch him ore of all,
Get all, pursse all, and be possest of all,
And then conclude the match, marrie, at least,
When, can you tell?"
Sig. D 3.

Act iii. sc. 2.

" Far more, far more, to you do I *decline.*"

Mr. Collier observes that this " may be reconciled to sense; but the reading of the corrector of the folio, 1632, ' *in*cline,' which makes a very trifling change, seems preferable." *Notes and Emendations,* &c. p. 61.

The Manuscript-corrector merely substituted a word more familiar to himself and those of his time than " decline." That the latter is what Shakespeare wrote, is not to be doubted: compare Greene; " That the loue of a father, as it was royall, so it ought to be impartiall, neither *declining* to the one nor to the other, but as deeds doe merite." *Penelope's Web,* sig. G 4, ed. 1601.

Act iii. sc. 2.

" *Dro. S.* Swart, like my shoe, but her face nothing like so clean kept : *for why?* she sweats ; a man may go over shoes in the grime of it."

So, in all editions, an interrogation-point is wrongly put after " why." The words ought to run,—"*for why* she sweats; a man," &c.,—"*for why*" being equivalent to *because, for this reason that.* Compare ;

" But let me see ; what time a day ist now ?
It cannot be imagin'd by the sunne,
For why I haue not seene it shine to daie," &c.
A Warning for Faire Women, 1599, sig. E 4.

> " Content he lies, and bathes him in the flame,
> And goes
> Not forth,
> *For why* he cannot liue without the same."
>
> Greene's *Neuer too late*, sig. P 2, ed. 1611.

> " Thomas, kneele downe ; and, if thou art resolu'd,
> I will absolue thee here from all thy sinnes,
> *For why* the deed is meritorious."
>
> *The Troublesome Raigne of King John* (*Part Sec.*), sig. L 2, ed. 1622.

Act iv. sc. 2.

" A devil in an everlasting garment hath him," &c.

The following description of a Sergeant is worth quoting, as it was drawn, no doubt, from the life : " One of them had on a buffe-leather jerkin, all greasie before with the droppings of beere that fell from his beard, and, by his side, a skeine like a brewers bung knife ; and muffled hee was in a cloke turn'd ouer his nose, as though hee had beene ashamed to shew his face." (We are afterwards told that he is a Sergeant.) Greene's *Quip for an Vpstart Courtier*, sig. D 3, ed. 1620.

Act iv. sc. 2.

> " Have you not heard men say,
> That Time comes stealing on by night and day?
> If *he* be in debt and theft, and a sergeant in the way,
> Hath he not reason to turn back an hour in a day?"

In the third line the old copies have " If *I* be in debt." Malone altered " *I* " to " he,"—which his successors adopt. Rowe read, " If *Time* be in debt," &c., and, I think, rightly: in the MS. used for the first folio, the word (because it had occurred so often just before) was probably written here contractedly, " T," which the compositor might easily mistake for " I."

Act iv. sc. 3.
" *Ant. S.* Avoid *then*, fiend."

" The manuscript-corrector of the folio, 1632, has it, ' Avoid, *thou* fiend!' which is probably accurate, but the change is trifling." Collier's *Notes and Emendations*, &c. p. 62.

Here the Manuscript-corrector has anticipated me. On the margin of the *Varior. Shakespeare*, I noted down what follows several years ago. " The word ' then' seems uncalled for by any thing that Dromio has just said: Antipholus had already declared that the lady was ' Satan' and ' the devil:'—surely, the right reading is '*Avoid* thee, *fiend!*'"

I must add,—first, that " thee" is preferable to " *thou*," because it comes nearer the old reading " then ;" and secondly, that " *Avoid* thee, *fiend!*" is much more common than " *Avoid*, thou *fiend!*" (the former occurs frequently even in modern writers; *e.g.*

" *Avoid thee, fiend!* with cruel hand
Shake not the dying sinner's sand," &c.
Scott's *Marmion*, c. vi.)

Act iv. sc. 4.
"*Ant. E.* You minion, you; are these your *customers?*"

" A *customer* is used in Othello for a common woman. *Here it seems to signify one who visits such women.*" MALONE.

This is the only note on the passage; and a surprising

note it is.—"*Your customers*" means nothing more than—the people who frequent your house. ("*Auentore, a customer*, a commer or a frequentor to a place." Florio's *Dict*.)

Act v. sc. 1.
" The place of *depth* and *sorry* execution.'
" Is amended in manuscript in the folio, 1632, to
' The place of *death* and *solemn* execution.'"
Collier's *Notes and Emendations*, &c. p. 63.

That "*depth*" was a misprint for "death," I did not require the authority of the Manuscript-corrector to convince me; but I am glad that he has pronounced it to be so, because the probability of any future editor retaining it is thereby considerably lessened. (Even Mr. Collier, who gave "death" in his text, was afterwards troubled with great doubts whether he had done rightly: see the "*Additional Notes*" to his *Shakespeare*, i. cclxxxv.)

According to Mr. Hunter, "'The place of *depth*' means, in the Greek story, the Barathrum, the deep pit, into which offenders were cast. So Jonson,—

'Opinion! let gross opinion sink
As deep as *Barathrum*.'
Every Man in his Humour, ed. 1601."
New Illustr. of Shakespeare, i. 225.

I do not perceive the appositeness of this quotation from Jonson.* In it "*Barathrum*" undoubtedly means *hell*. Compare Dekker's *Knights Conjuring*, 1607; "In-

---

* It is incorrectly cited above. In the quarto, 1601, it stands thus;
"Opinion, *O God* let grosse opinion sinck *and be damnd*
As deepe as Barathrum."
Sig. M.

raged at which, he flung away, and leapt into *Barathrum*."
Sig. c 3. Taylor's *Worlds Eighth Wonder;*

" Thus all blacke *Barathrum* is fill'd with games,
With lasting bone-fires, casting sulphur-flames."
p. 67,—*Workes*, ed. 1631.

and his *Bawd;*

" Cocitus Monarch, high and mighty Dis,
Who of Great Limbo-Lake Commander is,
Of Tartary, of Erebus, and all
Those Kingdomes which men Barathrum doe call."
p. 92 (second),—*Ibid.*

Act v. sc. 1.

" *Serv.* O mistress, mistress, shift and save yourself!
My master and his man are both broke loose,
Beaten the maids a-row, and bound the doctor,
Whose beard they have sing'd off with brands of fire;
And, ever as it blaz'd, they threw on him
Great pails of puddled mire to quench the hair :
My master preaches patience to him, and the while
His man with scissors nicks him like a fool.
* * * * * * * * *
Mistress, upon my life, I tell you true;
I have not breath'd almost, since I did see it.
He cries for you, and vows, if he can take you,
To *scorch* your face, and to disfigure you."

Warburton saw that, in the last line, the true reading was "scotch;" but this obvious emendation has been treated with contempt by his successors. " '*Scorch*,' says Steevens, " I believe, is right. He would have punished her as he had punished the conjurer before ;"— which must have been *by singing off her beard!*—The folio has the very same misprint in *Macbeth*, act iii. sc. 2;

" We have *scorch'd* [read " scotch'd"] the snake, not kill'd it."

So, too, have all the old editions of Beaumont and Fletcher's *Knight of the Burning Pestle*, act iii. sc. 4;

" *Re-enter* GEORGE, *leading a second* Man, *with a patch over his nose.*

 George. Puissant Knight, of the Burning Pestle hight,
See here another wretch, whom this foul beast
Hath *scorcht* [read "scotch'd"] and scor'd in this inhuman wise !"

    Act v. sc. 1.
  " I think, you all have drunk of Circe's cup."

Malone writes; " The Duke means to say, I think you all are out of your senses; so below;—

 ' I think you are all mated, or *stark* mad.'

Circe's potion, however, though it transformed the companions of Ulysses into swine, and deprived them of speech, did not, it should seem, deprive them of their reason; for Homer tells us that they lamented their transformation. However, the Duke's words are sufficiently intelligible, if we consider them as meaning—Methinks you all are become as irrational as beasts."

But Malone forgets Virgil; who evidently meant us to understand that those whom Circe had transformed were " deprived of reason;"

  " Hinc exaudiri gemitus iræque leonum,
   Vincla recusantum, et sera sub nocte rudentum ;

THE COMEDY OF ERRORS.   35

  Setigerique sues, atque in præsepibus ursi
  Sævire, ac formæ magnorum ululare luporum."
          Æn. vii. 15.

" Resembling those Grecians, that, with Vlysses, drinking of Circes drugges, lost both forme *and memorie.*" Greene's *Neuer too late,* sig. G 4, ed. 1611.

Act v. sc. 1.

" The following lines," says Mr. Collier, " as they are printed in the folio, 1623, have been the source of considerable cavil:

  ' Thirty-three years have I but gone in travail
  Of you, my sons, and till this present hour
  My heavy burden are delivered.'

That the above is corrupt there can be no question; and in the folio, 1632, the printer attempted thus to amend the passage:—

  ' Thirty-three years have I been gone in travail
  Of you, my sons; and till this present hour
  My heavy burdens are delivered.'

Malone gave it thus:—

  ' Twenty-five years have I but gone in travail
  Of you, my sons; until this present hour
  My heavy burden not delivered.'

The manuscript-corrector of the folio, 1632, makes the slightest possible change in the second line, and at once removes the whole difficulty: he puts it,—

> ' Thirty-three years have I been gone in travail
> Of you, my sons, and *at* this present hour
> My heavy burdens are delivered.' "
>
> *Notes and Emendations,* &c. p. 64.

I cannot think, with Mr. Collier, that, when the Manuscript-corrector alters "till" to "*at*," he "*makes the slightest possible change.*" The utter improbability that "*at*" should have been mistaken for "till" either by scribe or compositor, strongly warrants the belief that the latter word was really the poet's: and I must be allowed to repeat here what I formerly advanced in my *Remarks on Collier's and Knight's eds. of Shakespeare,* viz.;—"I have little doubt that the genuine text is,—

> ' and till this present hour
> My heavy burden *ne'er* delivered.'

Our early printers sometimes mistook '*ne'er*' (written *nere*) for *are.*" p. 30.

With respect to the first line of the passage, as it is given above with the *imprimatur* of the Manuscript-corrector,—

> "*Thirty-three* years have I *been* gone in travail,"—

Mr. Collier can hardly mean that "*Thirty-three*" is right, because the Manuscript-corrector has allowed that number to stand (see Theobald's note, or Mr. Collier's own note, ad l.); and surely we may more than suspect that "*been*" was arbitrarily substituted for "but" by the editor or printer of the second folio.

MUCH ADO ABOUT NOTHING.

Act i. sc. 1.

The quarto and the folio have "*Enter Leonato, gouernour of Messina,* Innogen his wife," &c. (and again at the commencement of Act ii. they make "his wife" enter with Leonato.) "It is therefore clear," says Mr. Collier ad l., "that the mother of Hero made her appearance before the audience, although she says nothing throughout the comedy;" and the same gentleman, in his *Notes and Emendations,* &c., remarks, that "the manuscript-corrector of the folio, 1632, has expunged the words *Innogen, his wife,* as if the practice had not then been for her to appear before the audience in this or in any other portion of the comedy." p. 66.

The great probability is, that *she never appeared before any audience in any part of the play*, and that Theobald was right when he conjectured that "the poet had in his first plan designed such a character, which, on a survey of it, he found would be superfluous, and therefore he left it out." One thing I hold for certain, viz. that, if she ever *did* figure among the dramatis personæ, it was not as a mere dummy: there are scenes in which the mother of Hero *must* have spoken;—she could not have stood on the stage without a word to say about the disgrace of her daughter, &c.

Act i. sc. 1.

"*Leon.* How many gentlemen have you lost in this action?
Mess. But few of *any sort*, and none of name."

According to Monck Mason, "of *any sort*" means—of any kind whatsoever; an interpretation which, though manifestly wrong, has found approvers. The reply of the Messenger is equivalent to—But few gentlemen of any rank, and none of celebrity. So presently he says to Beatrice, "I know none of that name, lady; there was none such in the army of *any sort*." So, too, in *Midsummer-Night's Dream*, act iii. sc. 2;

> "none of noble *sort*
> Would so offend a virgin:"

and in Jonson's *Every Man in his Humour,—Works*, i. 24, ed. Gifford; "A *gentleman of your sort*, parts," &c.: and in *A Warning for Faire Women*, 1599;

> "The Queene our mistris
> Allowes this bounty to all commers, much more
> To *gentlemen of your sort*."
> Sig. F 2.

Act i. sc. 1.

"or do you play the flouting Jack, to tell us Cupid is a good hare-finder, and Vulcan a rare carpenter?"

Mr. Knight prints "from two correspondents" an explanation of this passage,—which explanation he has no doubt is the right one. I am inclined to think so too. *But it was given long ago by Tollet.*

Act i. sc. 1.

"*Bene.* Like the old tale, my lord: it is not so, nor 'twas not so; but indeed God forbid it should be so."

Blakeway (see the *Varior. Shakespeare*) has preserved,

from the relation of his "great aunt," a very curious story, which may really be a modernised version of "*the old tale*" here alluded to: but he was not aware that one of the circumstances in the good lady's narrative is borrowed from Spenser's *Faerie Queene;*
"When she arrived at the house, and knocked at the door, no one answered. At length she opened it, and went in. Over the portal of the hall was written, *Be bold, be bold, but not too bold:* she advanced. Over the staircase, the same inscription: she went up. Over the entrance of a gallery, the same: she proceeded. Over the door of a chamber, *Be bold, be bold, but not too bold, lest that your heart's-blood should run cold,*" &c. Blakeway's Tale.

"And, as she lookt about, she did behold
How over that same dore was likewise writ,
Be bolde, be bolde, and every where, *Be bold;*
That much she muz'd, yet could not construe it
By any ridling skill or commune wit.
At last she spyde at that rowmes upper end
Another yron dore, on which was writ,
Be not too bold; whereto though she did bend
Her earnest minde, yet wist not what it might intend."
The Faerie Queene, B. iii. C. xi. st. 54.

Act i. sc. 1.

"*D. Pedro.* Nay, if Cupid have not spent all his quiver in Venice, thou wilt quake for this shortly."

Long before this comedy was produced, various writers had characterised Venice as the place where Cupid "reigns and revels." So Greene; "Hearing that of all the citties in Europe, Venice hath most semblance of Venus vanities .... Because therefore this great city of Venice is holden Loues Paradice," &c. *Neuer too late,* sig. Q 2, ed. 1611. —At a somewhat later period, Coryat's *Crudities* made the Venetian courtesans well known in England.

Act i. sc. 1.

" *Bene.* I have almost matter enough in me for such an embassage ; and so I commit you—

Claud. To the tuition of God : From my house (*if I had it*)—"

There is the same sort of joke in the translation of the *Menæchmi,* 1595, by W. W. [William Warner?];

" *Men.* What, mine owne Peniculus ?

Pen. Yours (ifaith), bodie and goods, *if I had any.*"

Sig. B.

Act i. sc. 3.

" *What is he for a fool* that betroths himself to unquietness ?"

I have elsewhere observed (*Remarks on Collier's and Knight's editions of Shakespeare,* p. 32) that " *What is he for a fool*" is equivalent to—What manner of fool is he,—What fool is he ?—So in Middleton's *A Mad World, my Masters;* " *What is she for a fool* would marry thee, a madman ?" *Works,* ii. 421, ed. Dyce. And compare Warner's *Syrinx,* &c.; "And *what art thou for a man* that thou shouldest be fastidious of the acquaintance of men ?" Sig. Q 4, ed. 1597.

Act ii. sc. 1.

" So deliver I up my apes, and away to Saint Peter *for the heavens: he shews me* where the bachelors sit, and there live we as merry as the day is long."

With the above very erroneous punctuation the passage stands in all the modern editions, except that of Mr. Knight, who properly follows the old copies in pointing it, "—and away to Saint Peter: *for the heavens, he shews me,*" &c. That "*for the heavens*" is nothing more than a petty oath has been proved by Gifford, Jonson's *Works,* ii. 68, vi. 333.

Act ii. sc. 1.

" *D. Pedro.* My visor is Philemon's roof; within the house is Jove.
Hero. Why, then your visor should be thatch'd.
D. Pedro. Speak low, if you speak love."

" Perhaps," says Blakeway, " the author meant here to introduce two of the long fourteen-syllable verses so common among our early dramatists, and the measure of Golding's translation [of Ovid]." Nobody, I should suppose, that has eyes and ears, could doubt it. But are the lines Shakespeare's own, or taken (at least partly) from some poem of the time which has perished? To me they read like a quotation.

Act ii. sc. 1.

" *Bene.* Well, I would you did like me!

F

Marg. So would not I, for your own sake; for I have many ill qualities.
Bene. Which is one?
Marg. I say my prayers aloud.
Bene. I love you the better; the hearers may cry, Amen.
Marg. God match me with a good dancer!
Balth. Amen.
Marg. And God keep him out of my sight, when the dance is done!—Answer, clerk.
Balth. No more words: the clerk is answered."

From a note in Mr. Knight's edition I learn that Tieck would give to Balthazar all the speeches in the above dialogue which are now assigned to Benedick; and several years before seeing that note, I had made, in my copy of the *Variorum Shakespeare,* the alteration which the German critic proposes. Mr. Knight remarks that, though Tieck is probably right, " still Benedick may first address Margaret, and then pass on, leaving Balthazar with her." I cannot think so. Benedick is now engaged with Beatrice, as is evident from what they presently say. Besides, —is not the effect of the scene considerably weakened,* if Benedick enters into conversation with any other woman except Beatrice?

Two prefixes, each beginning with the same letter, are frequently confounded by transcribers and printers: so, in *Love's Labour's lost,* act ii. sc. 1, *six speeches in succession* which belong to *Biron* are assigned in the folio to *Boyet.*

---

* Shortly before his death, Mr. Kenney the dramatist told me, that, having spent much time in examining each play of Shakespeare, scene by scene, merely with a view to ascertain what were its merits in point of construction, distribution of the dialogue, stage-effectiveness, &c., he had come to the conclusion that Shakespeare, even in the veriest minutiæ, was a consummate artist.

Indeed, we sometimes find in old plays such mistakes in the prefixes as it is impossible to account for: of this we have an instance in the present comedy, towards the close of which, the words, " Peace, I will stop your mouth,"— words that indubitably belong to *Benedick*,—are assigned, both in the quarto and in the folio, to *Leonato*.

Act ii. sc. 1.
" but *civil*, count, *civil* as an orange."

It may be noticed that a " *civil* (not a *Seville*) orange" was the orthography of the time. See Cotgrave's *Dict.* in "*Aigre-douce*" and in " *Orange*."

Act ii. sc. 3.
" *Enter* BENEDICK *and a* Boy."

Mr. Collier (ad l.) observes; " In the old copies Benedick enters ' alone' before the boy makes his appearance; and the reason is obvious, for Benedick should ruminate, and pace to and fro, before he calls the boy. In all the modern editions ' Benedick and a Boy' enter together: a very injudicious arrangement." Mr. Collier has accordingly given the opening of the scene thus;

" *Enter* BENEDICK.
Bene. Boy!
Enter a Boy.
Boy. Signior:"—

but probably, when Mr. Collier reprints his *Shakespeare,*

he will acquiesce in the modern arrangement, since the Manuscript-corrector of the folio, 1632, has added to the entrance of Benedick, "*Boy following*."—The truth is, the *entrances* of "such small deer" as *Pages* are frequently omitted in the old copies of plays. Compare Dekker's *Match me in London*, 1631, where a scene commences thus;

"*Enter Don John.*
Joh. Boy!
Pach. My lord?" &c.

p. 54 [55],—the entrance of the page Pacheco not being marked.

Act iii. sc. 2.

" he hath twice or thrice cut Cupid's bow-string, and the little *hangman* dare not shoot at him."

Farmer says that this character of Cupid is from Sidney's *Arcadia* (B. ii. p. 156, ed. 1598), where we are told that Jove appointed Cupid

"In this our world *a hangman* for to be
Of all those fooles that will have all they see."

Perhaps so. But I suspect that "*hangman*" is here equivalent to—rascal, rogue. (In Johnson's *Dict.* sub "*Hangman*," the present passage is cited to exemplify the word employed as a term of reproach.) It is at least certain that *hangman*, having come to signify an executioner in general—(so in Fletcher's *Prophetess*, act iii. sc. 1, Dioclesian, who had *stabbed* Aper, is called "*the hangman* of Volusius Aper;" and in *Jacke Drums Entertainement*, Brabant Junior, being prevented by Sir Edward from *stabbing himself*, declares that he is too wicked to live,—

> " And therefore, gentle knight, let mine owne hand
> Be mine own *hangman*."
>
> Sig. H 3, ed. 1616)—

was afterwards used as a general term of reproach (so in *Guy Earl of Warwick, a Tragedy*, printed in 1661, but acted much earlier; " Faith, I doubt you are some lying *hangman*," i. e. rascal).

Act v. sc. 1.
" And *made a push* at chance and sufferance."

This passage was misunderstood, till Mr. Collier explained " push" to be an interjection (a form of *pish*),— referring to some of my editions for examples of its use. I subjoin two others;

> " *Pem.* Deare friend—
> *Fer. Push*, meet me."
>
> *The Tryall of Cheualry*, 1605, sig. C 4.

" *Grac.* But I prithee practise some milder behauiour at the ordinarie, be not al madman.
Acut. Push, ile bee all obseruatiue," &c.

Everie Woman in her Humor, 1609, sig. E 2.

I may add;

" Well, jest on, gallants; and, vncle, you that *make a pish at* the Black Art," &c.

Day's *Law Trickes*, 1608, sig. I 2.

Act v. sc. 1.

"Scambling, out-facing, fashion-*mong'ring* boys."

Here Mr. Knight, alone of the modern editors, follows the old copies in printing " fashion-monging,"—and rightly, for instances of that form are not wanting in our early authors: so in Wilson's *Coblers Prophecie*, 1594;

" Then where will be the schollers allegories,
Where the Lawier with his dilatories,
Where the Courtier with his brauerie,
And the money-*monging* mate with all his knauerie ?"

Sig. B 3.

Act v. sc. 1.

" I will bid thee draw, as we do the minstrels."

"*As we bid the minstrels*" means, according to Malone, " draw the bows of their fiddles;" according to Mr. Collier, " draw their instruments out of their cases." The latter seems the more probable explanation: compare Dekker's *Satiromastix*, 1602 ; " Haue the merry knaues pul'd their fiddle cases ouer their instruments eares ?" Sig. B 2.

Act v. sc. 1.

" *Dog.* Come, you, sir; if justice cannot tame you, she shall ne'er weigh more *reasons* in her balance."

This quibble between *reasons* and *raisins* is found again in *Troilus and Cressida*, act ii. sc. 2. Indeed, it is as old as the time of Skelton, who says in his *Speke, Parrot;*

"Grete reysons with resons be now reprobitante,
For reysons ar no resons, but resons currant."
Works, ii. 22, ed. Dyce (where these lines were for the first time printed). See also Dekker's *Owles Almanacke*, 1618, sig. F 2.

Act v. sc. 2.
"I give thee the bucklers,"

i. e. I yield, lay aside all thoughts of defence. So Cotgrave, in his *Dict.* (sub *Gaigné*), has "*Je te le donne gaigné .... I giue thee the bucklers.*"

Act v. sc. 2.
"Yonder's *old coil* at home."

That, in such expressions, "*old*" is equivalent to "great, abundant," was never doubted, I suppose, by any one except the critic who reviewed my ed. of Beaumont and Fletcher in Churton's *Literary Register*.—Cotgrave, in his *Dict.*, has; "*Faire le diable de vauuert.* To play reaks, to keep an *old coile*, or horrible stirre." I know not if it has been observed that the Italians use (or at least formerly used) " vecchio" in the same sense;

"Perchè Corante abbandonava il freno,
E dette un *vecchio* colpo in sul terreno."
Pulci,—*Morg. Mag.* c. xv. st. 54.

" E so ch' egli ebbe di *vecchie* paure."
Id. c. xix. st. 30.

(It is rather remarkable that Florio, in his *Dict.*, has not given this meaning of " vecchio.")

LOVE'S LABOUR'S LOST.

Act i. sc. 1.

" *King.* Well, *sit* you *out:* go home, Biron, adieu."

In his note on these words Mr. Collier says, " The folio has '*fit* you out,' which may be right." Assuredly not: and, if the passage cited by Steevens from Bishop Sanderson be thought insufficient to shew that the quarto gives the true reading, here is another passage which puts the matter beyond all doubt;

" *Lewis.* . . . .
King of Nauar, will onely *you sit out?*
  Nau. No, King of Fraunce, my bloud's as hot as thine,
And this my weapon shall confirme my words."
The Tryall of Cheualry, 1605, sig. G 3.

Act i. sc. 1.

" *Biron.* How low soever the matter, I hope in God for high words.

Long. A high hope for a low *having:* God grant us patience!
Biron. To hear, or forbear *hearing?*
Long. To hear meekly, sir, and to laugh moderately; or to forbear both."

In this passage the old eds. give " A high hope for a low *heaven.*" Theobald (whose alteration has generally been adopted) substituted " having" for " *heaven.*"

From Mr. Collier's *Notes and Emendations*, p. 82, we learn that "the corrector of the folio, 1632, says that we ought to erase 'heaven' for *hearing* :—

'A high hope for a low *hearing:* God grant us patience!'

What Biron adds seems consequent upon it, when he asks whether the patience prayed for is to be granted, 'to hear, or to forbear *hearing.*'"

I shall not discuss the question whether Theobald's "having" be right or wrong (Mr. Collier, in his edition of *Shakespeare*, says, Theobald "was probably right;" in the *Notes and Emendations* he says, Theobald "was most likely wrong"). As to the Manuscript-corrector's emendation, "hearing,"—I strongly suspect that it was made merely in consequence of his finding that word in the next speech. But is "hearing" the right reading *in Biron's speech?* No; it is manifestly wrong: what immediately follows proves that it is a mistake of the scribe or the printer for "laughing,"—the excellent correction of Steevens, which Malone calls "plausible," and which the later editors do not even mention.

Act i. sc. 1.

"*Biron.* Well, sir, be it as the style shall give us cause to *climb* in the merriness."

"The manuscript-corrector has altered 'clime in the merriness' of the old copies, to '*chime in* in the merriness,' in allusion to the laughable contents expected in Armado's letter, 'in the merriness' of which the King and his companions hope to 'chime in' or participate." Collier's *Notes and Emendations*, &c. p. 82.

But we can hardly doubt that on the word "*style*" a quibble was intended, which is destroyed by the Manuscript-corrector's alteration. Compare, in act iv. sc. 1,—

"*Boyet.* I am much deceiv'd, but I remember *the style.*
Prin. Else your memory is bad, *going o'er it* erewhile."

So also, in Dekker's *Satiro-mastix,* 1602, Asinius Bubo, who has been reading a book, says of its author, " The whoorson made me meete with a hard *stile* in two or three places *as I went ouer him.*" Sig. c 4. And in Day's *Ile of Guls,* 1606; " But and you vsde such a high and eleuate *stile,* your auditories low and humble vnderstandings should neuer *crall ouer't.*" Sig. F.

Act ii. sc. 1.
" Now, madam, summon up your *dearest* spirits."

" To this line," says Mr. Collier (*Notes and Emendations,* &c. p. 83), " Steevens has appended a note in which he observes, that '*Dear,* in our author's language, has many shades of meaning: in the present instance and the next, it appears to signify, best, most powerful.' The fact is (if we may trust the corrector of the folio, 1632) that 'dearest' was a misprint for *clearest;* and it is easy to see how *cl* might be mistaken for *d.* He gives the line:—

' Now, madam, summon up your *clearest* spirits ;'

that is, her brightest and purest spirits, that the Princess might adequately discharge the important embassy entrusted to her by her father."

But we are *not* to " trust the corrector of the folio,

1632," when he rashly alters "dearest" to "*clearest*" only because, during his time, the former word had become rather obsolete in the sense which it bears here. That "dearest" is the true lection, and that Steevens explained it rightly, we have proof (if proof were required) in a line of Dekker, who applies to "spirits" an epithet synonymous with "dearest,"

"Call vp your *lustiest spirits;* the lady's come."
If it be not good, the Diuel is in it, 1612, sig. c 3.

Act ii. sc. 1.

"*Ros. No point*, with my knife."

The double negative of the French, with a quibble. (It occurs again in act v. sc. 2.) We occasionally meet with it in passages of our old plays where no quibble is intended. So in *Jack Drums Entertainment;*

"I will helpe you to a wench, Mounsieur.
Moun. No point, a burne childe feere de fire."
Sig. c. ed. 1616.

and in *The Wisdome of Doctor Dodypoll*, 1600; "Vat, you go leave a de bride? tis *no point* good fashion." Sig. D 2: and sometimes we find it when the speakers are Englishmen.

Act ii. sc. 1.

"*His tongue, all impatient to speak and not see,*
Did stumble with haste in his eye-sight to be;
All senses to that sense did make their repair,
To feel only looking on fairest of fair."

On the first line of this passage the following notes are found in the *Variorum Shakespeare:*—

"That is—his tongue being impatiently desirous to see as well as speak." JOHNSON.

"Although the expression in the text is extremely odd, I take the sense of it to be, that—his tongue envied the quickness of his eyes, and strove to be as rapid in its utterance, as they in their perception. *Edinburgh Magazine,* Nov. 1786." STEEVENS.

Now, it would be difficult to say which of these notes is least to the purpose. The context distinctly shews that the meaning is—His tongue, *not able to endure* the having merely the power of speaking without that of seeing.

Again, on the fourth line we find, *ibid.*:—

"Perhaps we may better read: 'To *feed* only *by* looking.'" JOHNSON.

There is no necessity for any alteration. The meaning is—That they might have no feeling but that of looking, &c.

Act iii. sc. 1.

"*Arm.* How hast thou purchased this experience?
Moth. By my *penny* of observation."

The old eds. have "*penne* of observation." Hanmer, whose reading has been adopted by all later editors, altered "*penne*" to "penny."—But the manuscript-corrector of the folio, 1632, reads, "By my *pain* of observation,"—that is, says Mr. Collier (*Notes and Emendations,* &c. p. 85), "by the pains he had taken in observing the characters of men and women. What most militates against this alteration is the figurative use of the word 'purchased,' for obtained, by Armado." Instead of " What *most militates against* this alteration," Mr. Collier ought to have said, " What *utterly annihilates* this alteration."

Act iii. sc. 1.
" Dread prince of *plackets.*"

Concerning "*placket,*" see Steevens's *Amnerian* note on *King Lear,* act iii. sc. 4 ; and *Dict. of Arch. and Prov. Words,* by Mr. Halliwell; who observes ; " Nares, Dyce, and other writers, tell us a *placket* generally signifies a petticoat, but their quotations do not bear out this opinion." I still think that in the quotations referred to, as well as in the present passage, "*placket*" is equivalent to petticoat. A writer of the age of Charles the Second uses "*plackets*" in the sense of *aprons* (perhaps of *petticoats*); " The word Love is a fig-leaf to cover the naked sense, a fashion brought up by Eve, the mother of jilts : she cuckolded her husband with the Serpent, then pretended to modesty, and fell a making *plackets* presently." Crowne's *Sir Courtly Nice,* act ii. p. 13, ed. 1685.

Act iv. sc. 1.
" A stand where you may make the *fairest* shoot.
 Prin. I thank my beauty, I am *fair* that shoot,
And thereupon thou speak'st the *fairest* shoot.
*   *   *   *   *   Not *fair?* alack for woe !
 For. Yes, madam, *fair.*
 Prin.   Nay, never paint me now :
Where *fair* is not, praise cannot mend the brow.
*   *   *   *   *   *   *   *

> *Fair* payment for foul words is more than due.
>   *For.* Nothing but *fair* is that which you inherit.
>   *Prin.* See, see! my beauty will be sav'd by merit.
> O, heresy in *fair*, fit for these days!
> A giving hand, though foul, shall have *fair* praise."

"The corrector of the folio, 1632, has it,—

> 'O, heresy in *faith*, fit for these days!'

which is probably right, although Shakespeare, like many other poets of his time, uses 'fair' for *fairness* or *beauty*." Collier's *Notes and Emendations*, &c. p. 87.

Surely the context proves the Manuscript-corrector to be altogether wrong. Here *fair** is, of course, equivalent to—beauty; in which sense Milton (though his editors do not notice it) uses the word in *Paradise Lost;*

> "no *fair* to thine
> Equivalent or second."
>
> Book ix. 608.

Act iv. sc. 2.

"*Dull.* If a *talent* be a claw, look how he claws him with a talent."

To the examples of *talent* used for *talon* the following may be added.

"Or buying armes of the herald, who giues them the

---

* Incredible as it may seem, the reviewer of my ed. of Beaumont and Fletcher, in a periodical called Churton's *Literary Register*, denied that *fair* ever meant—beauty. The following couplet in Sylvester's *Du Bartas* would be alone sufficient to determine that it did:

"Causing her sit in a rich easie chaire,
    Himselfe, at ease, views and reviews her *faire*" [the original having "ses diuines *beautez*"].   *Bethulia's Rescue*, p. 502, ed. 1641.

LOVE'S LABOUR'S LOST.   55

Lion without tongue, taile, or *talents*." Nash's *Pierce Pennilesse his Supplication*, sig. F 4, ed. 1595.

> " The Griffin halfe a bird, and halfe a beast,
> Strong-arm'd with mightie beak, *tallents*, and creast."
> Baxter's *Sir P. Sidneys Ourania*, 1606, sig. H.

> " A second Phœnix rise, of larger wing,
> Of stronger *talent*, of more dreadfull beake," &c.
> Dekker's *Whore of Babylon*, 1607, sig. F 2.

Act iv. sc. 3.

> " *Biron* [*aside*]. O rhymes are gards on wanton Cupid's hose;
> Disfigure not his *shape*."

So Mr. Collier in his edition of Shakespeare (from a MS. correction in Lord Ellesmere's copy of the first folio) for the misprint of the old copies, "shop."

" A question has been agitated whether we ought to read *shape* or *slop*. Theobald was in favour of *slop*, and his conjecture is confirmed by the corrector of the folio, 1632." *Notes and Emendations*, &c. p. 89.

I nevertheless am inclined to think that the right reading is "*shape;*" in the first place, because the poet would hardly have used the word *slop* immediately after *hose;* and secondly because, in Fletcher's *Beggars' Bush*, act v. sc. 1, the first folio has,—

> " who assur'd me, Florio
> Liv'd in some merchant's *shop*,"—

a misprint which, in the second folio, is properly altered to "shape."

(*Shape* was often anciently spelt *shap*,—a form occasionally found even in MSS. of Shakespeare's time: hence the greater probability of the word being mistaken by a compositor for *shop*.)

Act v. sc. 1.

" For what is inward between us, let it pass :—I do beseech thee, *remember thy courtesy ;*—I beseech thee, apparel thy head."

So the passage is given in all copies ancient and modern. Malone saw that the addition of the word " not" was absolutely necessary for the sense; and yet he did not venture to introduce it into the text! Nothing can be more evident than that Shakespeare wrote, "*remember* not *thy courtesy.*" Holofernes had taken off his hat; and Armado condescendingly says,—Don't stand on courtesy, apparel thy head.

Act v. sc. 2.

" A lady *wall'd about* with diamonds!"

It may be noticed that Marlowe, in his *Dido,* had made Ganymede describe himself as " *wall'd in* with eagle's wings." *Works,* ii. 366, ed. Dyce.

Act v. sc. 2.

" *Ros.* 'Ware pencils! *How?* let me not die your debtor," &c.

So the line stands in all editions.

I have no doubt that we ought to print, " 'Ware pencils, *ho!*"—the " how" of the early copies being merely the old spelling of "*ho*." It would be easy to adduce many instances of that spelling. So, in the last scene of *The Taming of a Shrew*, ed. 1594, the Tapster, finding Sly asleep, calls out, " What *how* [*i. e.* ho], Slie! awake for shame" (which in the later eds. is erroneously altered to " What *now*," &c.). So too in *The History of Stukeley*, 1605,

" Are the gates shut alreadie? open *how* [*i. e.* ho !]."
Sig. E 3.

and afterwards, " Some water, water *howe* [*i. e.* ho !]." Sig. L.

See also my remarks on *Anthony and Cleopatra*, act i. sc. 2, in this volume.

In the present passage "*ho*" is, of course, equivalent to *cease, stop*,—a meaning which formerly it often bore.

Act v. sc. 2.

"*King.* Farewell, mad wenches: you have simple wits.
Prin. Twenty adieus, my frozen *Muscovites*.
Exeunt King, Lords, &c."

So the modern editors. But they ought to have followed the old copies, which here (*and here only*) have, for the sake of exact rhyme, " Muscovits."

Those who are well read in our early poets will recollect the strange liberties which some of them take with words when a rhyme is required.

Act v. sc. 2.

" *Biron.* This jest is dry to me.—*Fair*, gentle *sweet*,
Your wit makes wise things foolish."

"*Fair*" (which Malone altered to "My," and which Mr. Knight rejects) is adopted from the second folio by Mr. Collier; and in all probability it was the word here used by Shakespeare. So in Day's *Law-Trickes*, 1608, we find, " God saue, *faire sweete*." Sig. B 4.

Act v. sc. 2.
" Judas was hang'd on an elder."

See Marlowe's *Jew of Malta* (and note), *Works*, i. 329, ed. Dyce.

Pulci has;

" Era di sopra a la fonte *un carrubbio*,
L' arbor, si dice, ove s' impiccò Giuda," &c.
Morgante Mag. c. xxv. st. 77.

Act v. sc. 2.
" *King*. The extreme *parts of time extremely form*
[the quarto and the folio " formes"]
All causes to the purpose of his speed;
And often, at his very *loose*, decides
That which long process could not arbitrate."

" The passage," observes Mr. Collier, " is corrupt, and the manuscript alteration made in the folio, 1632, thus sets it right, and renders the sense distinct;

' The extreme *parting* time *expressly forms*
All causes,' &c."
Notes and Emendations, &c. p. 96.

The Manuscript-corrector's alteration is ingenious: that it restores the original reading, I am far from convinced.

Strange to say, the commentators seem to have been puzzled by the word "*loose.*" The only note on that word in the *Variorum Shakespeare* is the following one;

"*At his very loose* may mean *at the moment of his parting, i. e.* of his *getting loose,* or away from us. So, in some ancient poem, of which I forgot to preserve either the date or title [the poem is Drayton's *Fifth Eglogue,* p. 449, ed. 1619];

' Envy discharging all her pois'nous [poys'ned] darts,
    The valiant mind is temper'd with that fire,
At her fierce *loose* that weakly never parts [starts],
    But in despight doth force her to retire.'"

STEEVENS.

Loose is properly the act of discharging an arrow; "the archers terme, who is not said to finish the feate of his shot before he giue the *loose,* and deliuer his arrow from his bow." Puttenham's *Arte of English Poesie,* 1589, p. 145. Compare *A Warning for Faire Women,* 1599;

" Twice, as you see, this sad distressed man,
    The onely marke whereat foule Murther shot,
Just in the *loose* of enuious eager Death,
    By accidents strange and miraculous,
Escap't the arrow aymed at his hart."

Sig. E 3.

and Beaumont and Fletcher's *Cupid's Revenge;*

" But he shall know ere long that my smart *loose*
Can thaw ice, and inflame the wither'd heart
Of Nestor."

Act ii. sc. 1.

In a famous passage of *Midsummer-Night's Dream* we have the verb,—"*loos'd*" (on which the commentators give no note);

> " And *loos'd* his love-shaft smartly from his bow,
> As it should pierce a hundred thousand hearts."
>
> Act ii. sc. 2.

"*Descocher une fleiche.* To shoote, *loosse*, or send an arrow from a bow." Cotgrave's *Dict.*

A MIDSUMMER-NIGHT'S DREAM.

Act i. sc. 2.

" I could play Ercles rarely, or a part to tear a cat in, to *make all split.*"

The expression "*make all split,*" and the similar one, "*let all split,*" are often met with in early writers.—It has not, I believe, been remarked that they are properly nautical phrases: " He set downe this period with such a sigh, that, *as the Marriners say*, a man would haue thought *al would have split* againe." Greene's *Neuer too late*, sig. G 3, ed. 1611.

Act ii. sc. 1.

" The cowslips *tall* her pensioners be;
In their gold *coats* spots you see," &c.

The Manuscript-corrector of the folio, 1632, alters "*tall*" to " all," and " coats" to " *cups.*" See *Notes and Emendations*, &c. p. 100.

The second of these alterations may be right. But the first is more than questionable; and when Mr. Collier defended it by observing that " cowslips are never ' tall,' " he ought to have considered, that, however diminutive they may appear to himself, as he gathers them in those sylvan scenes to which (unfortunately for his friends and acquaintances) he has now withdrawn, they might nevertheless seem "tall" to Titania and her elves in the Athenian forest; just as the *tulip* was "*lofty*" to certain other fairies, who held their revels in Kensington Gardens, before nature (or rather art) had produced people of fashion;

"Beneath *a lofty tulip's ample shade*
Sat the young lover and th' immortal maid."*

In a note on the present passage of Shakespeare, the following stanza from Drayton's *Nymphidia* is not inaptly cited by Johnson;

"And for the Queen *a fitting bower*,
Quoth he, is that fair *cowslip-flower*,
On Hipcut-hill that groweth;
In all your train there's not a fay
That ever went to gather May,
But she hath made it in her way
The *tallest* there that groweth."

Act iv. sc. 1.

"Her dotage now I do begin to pity;
For meeting her of late, behind the wood,
Seeking sweet *savours* for this hateful fool," &c.

So Malone, Mr. Knight, and Mr. Collier, read with the folio and Roberts's quarto. The other quarto has "favours;" which (though Mr. Collier says "'*savours*' seems preferable") I think decidedly right. Titania was

* Tickell's *Kensington Gardens*.

seeking flowers for Bottom to wear as *favours:* compare Greene; " These [fair women] with syren-like allurement so entised these quaint squires, that they bestowed all their *flowers* vpon them for *fauours.*" *Quip for an Vpstart Courtier,* sig. B 2, ed. 1620.

THE MERCHANT OF VENICE.

Act ii. sc. 5.

"*Fast bind, fast find;*
A proverb never stale in thrifty mind."

" The proverb with which the speech ends is given [by the Manuscript-corrector of the folio, 1632] differently both from quartos and folios; for instead of 'Fast bind, fast find,' we have '*Safe* bind, *Safe* find.'" Collier's *Notes and Emendations,* &c. p. 115.

The Manuscript-corrector seems to have made the change "for variation's sake."—Compare Cotgrave's *Dict.* sub *Bon.* "*Bon guet chasse malaventure:* Pro. Good watch preuents misfortune; *fast bind, fast find,* say we."

Act ii. sc. 9.

"*Enter a Messenger.*

Mess. Where is *my lady?*
Por. Here: what would *my lord?*"

Mr. Collier, in his ed. of *Shakespeare,* having observed, " It is clear that he [the Messenger] was not a mere servant, not only from the language put into his mouth, but because, when he asks, 'Where is my lady?' Portia replies, 'Here; what would my lord?' The Messenger was a person of rank attending on Portia,"—I maintained that the reply of Portia was nothing more than a sportive rejoinder to the abrupt exclamation of the Messenger, and I cited similar passages from Shakespeare's *First Part of Henry IV.* act ii. sc. 4, and from his *Richard II.* act v. sc. 5 (*Remarks on Collier's and Knight's editions of Shakespeare*, p. 55). I have since found the same sort of pleasantry in another dramatist;

> "*Enter Peter with a candle.*
> Pe. *Where* are you, *my Lord?*
> Hog. *Here, my Lady.*"
> *The Hogge hath lost his Pearle,* by R. Tailor, 1614, sig. H.

Act iii. sc. 1.

> " it was my *turquoise.*"

"Men," says Greene, "weare not jems onely to please the sight, but to be defensiues by their secret operations against perils." *Farewell to Follie,* sig. B 2, ed. 1617: and Steevens's note has made it plain that Shylock valued his turquoise, not only as being the gift of Leah, but on account of the imaginary virtues ascribed to the stone. The following lines of Donne may be added to Steevens's illustrations of the passage;

> " As a compassionate *Turcoyse,* which doth tell,
> By looking pale, the wearer is not well."
> *Anat. of the World,*—*Poems,* p. 247, ed. 1633.

Act v. sc. 1.

> " look, how the floor of heaven
> Is thick inlaid with *patterns* of bright gold."

So Mr. Collier in his *Shakespeare,* adopting the reading of the second folio. That of the first folio, and of Heyes's quarto, is " pattens." The other quarto has " pattents."

Though Mr. Hunter (*New Illustr. of Shakespeare,* i. 318) says, that " the constellations may not unsuitably be spoken of as *patterns,* just as we speak of the pattern of mosaic work, or the pattern of a flowered or spotted damask," I still think (see my *Remarks on Collier's and Knight's editions of Shakespeare,* p. 59) that " patterns" is a gross misprint, and that we must undoubtedly read " patines," or " pattens," or " pattents" (it matters little which; see Coles's *English-Latin Dict.* in " Patine ;" Todd's Johnson's *Dict.* in " Paten ;" and, for an example of "pattent," Hunter's *New Illust. of Shakespeare,* ii. 349).

The poet means that the floor of heaven is thickly inlaid with plates, or circular ornaments, of bright gold. Compare Sylvester's *Du Bartas;*

" Th' Almighties finger fixed many a million
Of *golden scutchions* [the original has "*platines dorees*"] in that
   rich pavillion."
The Fourth Day of the First Week, p. 33, ed. 1641.

" That sumptuous canapy,
The which th' un-niggard hand of Majesty
Poudred so *thick with shields* [the original has " *escussons*"] so
   shining cleer," &c.
Id. p. 34.

Act v. sc. 1.

" *the moon sleeps with Endymion.*"

The very same words occur in a writer with whose works Shakespeare, we know, was well acquainted;

"*The moon sleeps with Endymion* every day."
Marlowe's *Ovid's Elegies,—Works*, iii. 136, ed. Dyce.

AS YOU LIKE IT.

Act iii. sc. 5.

" The common executioner,
Whose heart th' accustom'd sight of death makes hard,
Falls not the axe upon the humbled neck,
But first begs pardon: will you sterner be
Than he that *dies* and lives by bloody drops ?"

" Perhaps ' dies' is to be taken in the sense of causes to die; but the corrector of the folio, 1632, removes all doubt, if we may take his representation of the original text, by substituting *kills*. . . . Can *dines* have been²the true word?" Collier's *Notes and Emendations,* &c. p. 134.

The old text must be right, because "dies" is evidently put in opposition to "lives;" and the Manuscript-corrector's alteration must be wrong, because it destroys the antithesis.

"I am afraid," says Steevens, " our bard is at his quibbles again. To *die* means as well *to dip a thing in a colour foreign to its own,* as to *expire*. In this sense, contemptible as it is, the executioner may be said to *die* as well as *live* by *bloody drops:*" and he adduces from early writers several instances of quibbles on the word *die*.

I am strongly inclined to agree with Steevens. In the following passage (which escaped his notice) " dying" seems to be used just as Shakespeare, according to the above explanation, has used "dies" (for we can hardly understand " dying" as equivalent either to *the dying of others* or to *causing to die*);

"Turbine the Dyer stalkes before his dore,
  Like Cæsar, that by *Dying* oft did thriue;
And though the Beggar be as proud as poore,
  Yet (like the mortifide) he dyes to liue."
      Davies's *Scourge of Folly*, 1611, *Epig.* 273.

Act v. sc. 4.
"His crown bequeathing to his banish'd brother,
And all their lands restor'd to *him* again
That were with him exil'd."

So the old copies.

The Manuscript-corrector " also introduces an emendation into the last line but two of the Second Brother's speech:—

'restor'd to *them* again
That were with him exil'd.'

The old text is 'him' for *them*, which may by ingenuity be reconciled to propriety; but *them* makes the passage more easily understood, which here, at least, in the winding up of the plot, must have been a main object with the poet." Collier's *Notes and Emendations*, &c. p. 140.

Mr. Collier will excuse me when I say that this is not the only part of his book which is calculated to mislead the reader. Who would not suppose, from the language used above, that the lection "*them*" was now for the first time brought forward? The fact is, that, Mr. Collier alone excepted, every recent editor has printed "them," without even thinking it necessary to notice the obvious misprint of the old copies.

THE TAMING OF THE SHREW.

Induction, sc. 1.
" Go by, *S*. Jeronimy."

" Sly's exclamation from ' The Spanish Tragedy,' ' Go by, S. Jeronimy,' has given commentators some trouble, in consequence of the capital S. before ' Jeronimy.' It seems to be merely a printer's blunder (who might fancy that St. Jerome was alluded to), and so the old corrector treated it, by unceremoniously putting his pen through it." Collier's *Notes and Emendations*, &c. p. 141.

But is the Manuscript-corrector to be justified in treating the " S." so unceremoniously? See my *Remarks on Collier's and Knight's editions of Shakespeare*, p. 65.

Act i. sc. 1.
" Or so devote to Aristotle's *checks*."

" What are ' Aristotle's checks?' Undoubtedly a misprint for Aristotle's *Ethics*, formerly spelt *ethicks*, and hence the absurd blunder" [which the Manuscript-corrector of the folio, 1632, sets right]. Collier's *Notes and Emendations*, &c. p. 144. See also " Introduction" to that volume, p. xi.

Blackstone conjectured " ethics" many years ago; since which time the whole reading world,—with the exception of Shakespeare's editors,—has been convinced that it is the true lection.

THE TAMING OF THE SHREW.

Act iv. sc. 2.
" I spied
An ancient *angel* coming down the hill."

" The word 'angel' has produced various conjectural emendations, the one usually adopted being that of Theobald, who proposed to read 'ancient *engle*;' but we are to recollect that the person spoken of was on foot, and we have no doubt that the word wanting [wanted?] is *ambler*, which we meet with in the margin of the corrected folio, 1632. As to *engle* or *ingle*, which means a person of weak understanding, how was Biondello to know that 'the Pedant' was so, by merely seeing him walk down the hill? he could see at once that he was an *ambler*. How *ambler* came to be misprinted 'angel' is a difficulty of perpetual recurrence." Collier's *Notes and Emendations*, &c. p. 151.

I never felt quite satisfied with the emendation " enghle" (ingeniously as it is supported by Gifford, note on B. Jonson's *Works*, ii. 430); nor does that of the Manuscript-corrector appear to me so certain as it does to Mr. Collier.

After all, is " *angel*" the right reading (though not in the sense of *messenger*, which is quite unsuited to the passage),—" *an ancient angel*" being equivalent to *an ancient worthy*, or simply to *an old fellow?* I must not be understood as answering this query in the affirmative when I cite from Cotgrave's *Dict.* " *Angelot à la grosse escaille. An old Angell;* and by metaphor, a fellow of th' old, sound, honest, and worthie stamp."

ALL'S WELL THAT ENDS WELL.

Act i. sc. 3.

" *Diana, no* queen of virgins, that would suffer her poor knight *to be* surprised, without rescue, in the first assault, or ransom afterward."

The words " Diana, no" and " to be" were supplied by Theobald, and have been adopted by all succeeding editors.

In my *Remarks on Collier's and Knight's editions of Shakespeare*, p. 69, I cited a passage from Drayton, in support of my assertion that Theobald had unnecessarily introduced the words " to be." That quotation, I understand, has been considered as insufficient to settle the point; and I now subjoin three other passages, which will leave no doubt in the mind of any reader that, according to the phraseology of our early authors, " to be" is a superfluous addition.

" If I in this his regall royall raigne
Without repulse should *suffer him remaine*."
King Carassus,—A Mirrour for Magistrates, p. 188, ed. 1610.

" By which her fruitful vine and wholesome fare
She *suffer'd spoil'd*, to make a childish snare."
Marlowe's *Hero and Leander,—Works*, iii. 61, ed. Dyce.

" Least we should be spotted with the staine of ingratitude, in *suffering the princesse iniury vnreuenged*."
Greene's *Penelope's Web*, sig. D 3, ed. 1601.

ALL'S WELL THAT ENDS WELL.

Act ii. sc. 1.

" *Hel.* What I can do, can do no hurt to try,
Since you set up your rest 'gainst remedy.
He that of greatest works is finisher,
Oft does them by the weakest minister:
So holy writ in babes hath judgment shown,
When judges have been babes. Great floods have flown
From simple sources; and great seas have dried,
When miracles have by the greatest been denied.
Oft expectation fails, and most oft there
Where most it promises; and oft it hits,
Where hope is coldest, and despair most *shifts.*"

In the last line the misprint of the old copies, "shifts," was altered by Pope to "*sits.*" Mr. Collier in his edition of *Shakespeare* gave "*fits,*" from a manuscript correction in a copy of the first folio belonging to Lord Ellesmere: "*fits*" is also the reading of the Manuscript-corrector of the folio, 1632; and doubtless the true one.

Mr. Knight puts back into the text the long-discarded "shifts;" and, after telling us that it means "resorts to expedients, depends upon chances, catches at straws,"—he proceeds thus; " Why, then, should not the word stand? A rhyme, it is said, is required to *hits.* Is it so? Have we a rhyme to this line?—

' Oft expectation fails, and most oft there.'

The couplets are dropped; and we have three lines of blank verse. As well that as *one* line without a corresponding line." Now, if Mr. Knight had been more familiar with our early dramatists, he would have known that, in such speeches, " *one* line without a corresponding line" is not unusual, just before the closing couplet. So

K

in *The Travailes of the Three Shirleys*, 1607, by Day, W. Rowley, and Wilkins;

> " Good mindes know this, imprisonment's no shame,
> Vnlesse the cause be foule which blots the name.
> Then all the griefes in my remembrance bee,
> Is that my father's eyes should weepe for mee
> And my misfortune: for mine owne mishapps
> Are to my minde as are heauen's thunder-claps,
> *Who cleares the ayre of fowle infection,*
> And in my thoughts do onely publish this,
> Affliction's due to man as life and sin is."
>
> Sig. G 4.

Act v. sc. 3.

" *Count.* Which better than the first, O dear Heaven, bless!
Or, ere they meet, in me, O nature, *cesse!*"

So the folio. Malone and Mr. Collier print " cease;" and we may well wonder that they should have rejected the older form of the word for one which destroys the rhyme. Mr. Knight rightly retains " *cesse,*" and quotes an instance of it from Chaucer's *Troilus and Cressida,*—which is going rather too far back: the fact is, Shakespeare found it in various works that were to him of recent date. E. g. in Phaer and Twyne's *Æneidos;*

> " This spoken, with a thought he makes the swelling seas to *cesse,*
> And sunne to shine, and clouds to flee, that did the skies oppresse."
>
> B. I. Sig. B iii. ed. 1584.

TWELFTH-NIGHT.

Act i. sc. 3.

"*Sir And.* Ay, 'tis strong, and it does indifferent well in a *flame-coloured* stock."

"Pope was wrong in his change respecting 'flame-colour'd stock:' the old editions have it '*dam'd* colour'd stock,' which the manuscript-corrector informs us ought to be '*dun*-colour'd stock.'" Collier's *Notes and Emendations*, &c. p. 172.

But it does not follow that "Pope was *wrong*," because the Manuscript-corrector hit on an alteration different from his. (When, in a passage of this very play, act ii. sc. 5, "And with what wing the *stallion* checks at it," the Manuscript-corrector substitutes "*falcon*" for "stallion," Mr. Collier, I presume, will allow that there at least he is quite "*wrong*," and that Hanmer, who conjectures "stannyel," is perfectly right.) That Sir Andrew, a gallant of the first water, should ever dream of casing his leg in a "*dun*-coloured stock," is not to be supposed for a moment.

The epithet "*flame-coloured*" was frequently applied to dress. In our author's *Henry IV. Part First*, act i. sc. 2, mention is made of a "wench in *flame-coloured* taffeta;" in *The Enventorey of all the aparell of the Lord Admeralles men, taken the* 13*th of Marche,* 1598, we find, "j *flame collerde* dublet pynked." Malone's *Shakespeare* (by Boswell), iii. 315; and in Nabbes's *Microcosmus* (see the *Dram. Pers.*) both Fire and Love wear "*flame-coloured*" habits.

Act iii. sc. 4.

"*Oli.* I have said too much unto a heart of stone,
And *laid* mine honour too unchary *out.*"

In this passage "out" is Theobald's correction for "on't" of the old editions,—a correction adopted by all succeeding editors, except Mr. Collier and Mr. Knight. Mr. Collier's note is; " ON'T] *i. e.* On the heart of stone: 'bestowed my honour too incautiously on a heart of stone.' Theobald changed 'on't' to *out,* but without reason." Mr. Knight's is; "*Unchary on't.* So in the original. The ordinary reading is '*unchary out.*' Douce is unwilling, as we are, to disturb the old reading. Olivia has laid her honour too unchary (uncharily) upon a heart of stone."

Though what I say will perhaps carry little weight with Mr. Collier, because I did not happen to exist about the year 1632; and though Mr. Knight is averse to the voice of criticism, whether it proceeds from the living or the dead;—I must yet exclaim against their thrusting back into the text an obvious error of the press.

The misprint of "on't" for "*out*" is common enough. So the quarto 1640 of Fletcher's *Bloody Brother,* act iv. sc. 1, has,—

"Princes may pick their suffering nobles *on't,*
And one by one employ them to the block," &c.—

where the other old copies have, as the sense requires, "*out.*" So, too, in Fletcher and Shakespeare's *Two Noble Kinsmen,* act i. sc. 4, the quarto 1634 has " Y'are *ont* of breath," where the second folio (the play is not in the first folio) gives "*out.*"

With the passage of Shakespeare now under consideration compare the following lines by a nameless dramatist;

"Keepe her from the Serpent, let her not gad
To euerie Gossips congregation,
For there is blushing modestie *laide out*," &c.
Euerie Woman in her Humor, 1609, sig. H 3.

Act v. sc. 1.

" *Clo.* Marry, sir, *lullaby* to your bounty, till I come again."

In *The Shakespeare Society's Papers*, vol. iii. 35, Mr. Halliwell observes that "*lullaby* is sufficiently unusual as a verb to justify an example;" and he adduces one. Here is another;

"Sweet sound that all mens sences *lullabieth.*"
Anthony Copley's *Fig for Fortune*, 1596, p. 59.

Act v. sc. 1.
" *Re-enter* FABIAN *with* MALVOLIO."

" When Malvolio is brought upon the scene by Fabian, we meet with a very particular stage-direction, obedience to which must have been intended to produce a ludicrous effect upon the audience: *Enter Malvolio, as from prison, with straw about him;* in order to show the nature of the confinement to which the poor conceited victim had been subjected." Collier's *Notes and Emendations,* &c. p. 180.

On the modern stage, Malvolio, in this scene, always enters with some " straw about him;" and such probably has been the invariable custom since the play was first produced. I well remember that, when *Twelfth-Night* was revived at Edinburgh* many years ago, Terry, who then acted Malvolio (and acted it much better than any one I have since seen in the part) had "straw about him," on his release from durance: nor is the straw omitted by the present representative of Malvolio at the Princess's Theatre.

* That revival is immortalised by Sir W. Scott: " Flora Mac-Ivor bore a most striking resemblance to her brother Fergus; so much so, that they might have played Viola and Sebastian, with the same exquisite effect produced by the appearance of Mrs. Henry Siddons and her brother [William Murray] in those characters." *Waverley*, vol. i. 317, third ed., 1814.

THE WINTER'S TALE.

Act i. sc. 2.

"*Leon. To bide upon't,*—thou art not honest; or,
If thou inclin'st that way," &c.

Here "*To bide upon't*" is equivalent to—My abiding opinion is. Compare Beaumont and Fletcher's *King and No King*, act iv. sc. 3;

"Captain, thou art a valiant gentleman;
To abide upon't, a very valiant man:"

and Potts's *Discoverie of Witches in the Countie of Lancaster*, 1613; "the wife of the said Peter then said, *to abide upon it*, I thinke that my husband will neuer mend," &c. Sig. T 4.

Act iv. sc. 3.

"O Proserpina,
For the flowers now, that, frighted, thou let'st fall
From *Dis's waggon!*"

(*i. e. Dis's chariot.*)

So Barnaby Barnes in his *Divils Charter*, 1607 (which in all probability preceded *The Winter's Tale*);

"From the pale horror of eternall fire
Am I sent with the *wagon of* blacke *Dis*," &c.
Sig. M 2.

Act iv. sc. 3.

"*Pol.* This is the prettiest low-born lass, that ever
Ran on the *green-sord.*"

So all the old copies. The modern editors print "*green-sward;*" but the other was undoubtedly Shakespeare's form of the word. Milton also wrote it "*sord;*"

"I' the midst an altar as the land-mark stood,
Rustic, of grassy *sord.*"
Par. Lost, xi. 433.

(where Fenton substituted "sod;" but Newton and Todd restored the old reading.)

And Pope, in one of his earliest pieces, has,—

"So featly tript the light-foot ladies round,
The knights so nimbly o'er the *greensword* bound," &c.
January and May,—(Tonson's *Miscellany*, 1709, vol. vi., where it originally appeared).

Coles, in his *English-Latin Dict.* (sub *Sword*), gives; "The green *sword, Cespes.*"

Act v. sc. 3.

"*Leon.* Let be, let be!
Would I were dead, but that, methinks, already—
What was he that did make it?—See, my lord,
Would you not deem it breath'd, and that those veins
Did verily bear blood?"

"One of those highly-important completions of the old, and imperfect, text of Shakespeare, consisting of a whole line, where the sense is left unfinished without it, here occurs. Warburton saw that something was wanting, but in note 3 it is suggested that Leontes in his ecstasy might have left his sentence unfinished: such does not appear to have been the case. . . . . [The Manuscript-corrector of the folio, 1632] thus supplies a missing line, which we have printed in Italic type:—

' Let be, let be !
Would I were dead, but that, methinks, already
I am but dead, stone looking upon stone.
What was he that did make it?' &c.

But for this piece of evidence, that so important an omission had been made by the old printer, or by the copyist of the manuscript for the printer's use, it might have been urged, &c. . . . However, we see above, that a line was wanting, and we may be thankful that it has been furnished, since it adds much to the force and clearness of the speech of Leontes." Collier's *Notes and Emendations,* &c. p. 197.

Mr. Collier is mistaken in saying that Warburton considered the text as defective: Warburton's note runs thus; "The sentence completed is;

'—but that, methinks, already I converse with the dead.'

But there his passion made him break off." Still, there is room to suspect that something has dropt out: and, on first reading the new line,—

" *I am but dead, stone looking upon stone,*"—

it appeared to me so exactly *in the style of Shakespeare,* that, like Mr. Collier, I felt "thankful that it had been furnished." But presently I found that it was *too Shakespearian.*

Only a few speeches before, Leontes has exclaimed;

> " O, thus she stood,
> Even with such life of majesty (warm life,
> As now it coldly stands), when first I woo'd her.
> I am asham'd: *does not the stone rebuke me,*
> *For being more stone than it?*—O royal piece,
> There's magic in thy majesty, which has
> My evils conjur'd to remembrance, and
> From thy admiring daughter took the spirits,
> *Standing like stone with thee!*"

Now, which is the greater probability?—that Shakespeare (whose variety of expression was inexhaustible) *repeated himself* in the line,—

> "*I am but dead, stone looking upon stone*"?

or that a reviser of the play (with an eye to the passage just cited) ingeniously constructed the said line, to fill up a supposed lacuna? The answer is obvious.

KING JOHN.

Act i. sc. 1.

" With that *half-face* would he have half my land."

In my *Remarks on Collier's and Knight's eds. of Shakepeare*, p. 87, I endeavoured to shew that Mr. Collier had injudiciously retained the reading of the old copies,—

" With *half* that *face* would he have half my land,"—

and I urged that "*half* that *face*" was merely a transposition made by a mistake of the original compositor. To what I have there said, let me add,—that a question in Fletcher's *Love's Pilgrimage*, act ii. sc. 4,—

" Where's the falconer's *half-dog* he left ?"

stands thus nonsensically in the first folio, by an accidental transposition,—

" Where's the *half* Falconer's *dog* he left ?"

Act i. sc. 1.

" *Lady F.* King Richard Cœur-de-lion was thy father;
By long and vehement suit I was seduc'd
To make room for him in my husband's bed:—
Heaven lay not my transgression to my charge!—
Thou art the issue of my dear offence,
Which was so strongly urg'd, past my defence."

So the passage used to be read from the time of Rowe (who, in the last line but one, altered " *That* art" of the old copies to " *Thou* art"), till Mr. Knight and Mr. Collier published their editions, where the close is exhibited thus;

" Heaven! [*the folios have no point here*] lay not my transgression to my charge,
   That art the issue of my dear offence," &c.

" Lady Faulconbridge," observes Mr. Knight, " *is not invoking Heaven to pardon her transgression;* but she says to her son,—for Heaven's sake, lay not (thou) my transgression to my charge that art the issue of it." Mr. Collier's explanation makes the old lady less of a hardened sinner: according to him, she means; " Let not heaven and you, *that art* the issue of my dear offence, lay the transgression to my charge." Mr. Knight thinks that the reading of the old copy is " in Shakespeare's manner ;" Mr. Collier that " no alteration is required."

That these gentlemen should ever have been able to satisfy themselves with such interpretations,—that Mr. Knight should have brought himself to believe that

" Heaven! lay not my transgression to my charge"

could signify, " *For heaven's* sake, lay not *thou* my transgression to my charge," and Mr. Collier seriously to opine that it was equivalent to " *Let not heaven and you* lay," &c.,—is to me a matter of downright astonishment.

No words were more frequently confounded by our early compositors than " thou" and " that." The reason is obvious:—" thou" was often written " y̆," and " that" often written " y̓." (We frequently find those abbreviated forms preserved in print: so the first folio has, in the present tragedy,—

"*Eng.* France, y̎ shalt rue this houre within this houre.
Bast. Old Time the clocke setter, ý bald sexton Time," &c.
Act iii. sc. 1.)

Act ii. sc. 1.

" Even till that England, *hedg'd in with the main*," &c.

Compare Greene's *Spanish Masquerado,* 1589; "Seeing how secure we [*i. e.* the English] slept . . . . . . for that wee were *hedged in with the sea*," &c.   Sig. B 4.

Act ii. sc. 1.

" All preparation for a bloody siege,
And merciless proceeding by these French,
Comfort your city's eyes," &c.

So the old copies.—" It has been urged by those who wished to adhere to the text of the folios, as long as it was unimpugned by any old authority, that ' comfort' was here used ironically: Rowe did not think so, when he printed *confront;* but the corrector of the folio, 1632, with less violence, has—

' *Come 'fore* your city's eyes,' &c."
Collier's *Notes and Emendations,* &c. p. 202.

It is to be hoped that no future editor will reject the certain emendation of Rowe for one, which, if it had been proposed by a critic of the present day, would have met with deserved contempt.

As to "*comfort*" being "used ironically," see my *Remarks on Collier's and Knight's eds. of Shakespeare*, p. 88.

Act ii. sc. 2.

"*K. John.* France, hast thou yet more blood to cast away? Say, shall the current of our right *roam* on," &c.

So Malone, Mr. Collier, and Mr. Knight,—because the first folio has "*rome.*" But "*rome*" is manifestly a misprint for "runne" (or perhaps for "ronne," as the MS. might have had that spelling); and the editor of the second folio rightly substituted "run." Steevens justly remarks; "The King would rather describe his right as *running on* in a *direct* than in an *irregular* course, such as would be implied by the word *roam*." (In this play the first folio is not uniform in the spelling of *run;* but it has "*runnes* tickling vp and downe," act iii. sc. 3; "when we haue *runne* so ill," act iii. sc. 4; "*runne* to meet displeasure," act v. sc. 1.)

Act iii. sc. 1.

"*Cons.* O Lewis, stand fast! the devil tempts thee here, In likeness of a new *untrimmed* bride."

On the word "*untrimmed*," how have the commentators written! how have I myself written! how foolishly, all of us!

I now see* (and with wonder at my former blindness) that nothing more is required than the change of a single letter,—that, *beyond the possibility of doubt*, Shakespeare wrote,—

"In likeness of a new u*p*-trimmed bride."

Compare what he elsewhere says *of a bride;*

"Go, waken Juliet; go, and *trim* her *up.*"
Romeo and Juliet, act iv. sc. 4.

So too Marlowe ;

"But by her glass disdainful pride she learns,
Nor she herself, but first *trimm'd up*, discerns."
Ovid's Elegies,— *Works,* iii. 174, ed. Dyce.

Act iii. sc. 3.

"If the midnight bell
Did, with his iron tongue and brazen mouth,
Sound *on* into the drowsy *race* of night."

So the old copies.
"The folio, 1632, as amended, has,—

'Sound on into the drowsy *ear* of night,'

instead of 'race of night,' as it stands in the folios : when 'ear' was spelt *eare,* as was most frequently the case, the mistake was easy, and we may now be pretty sure that 'race' was a mistake." Collier's *Notes and Emendations,* &c. p. 205.

Whether the emendation "ear" originated with the

* This emendation was mentioned as mine by Mr. Singer in *Notes and Queries* for July 3d, 1852.

Manuscript-corrector, or whether he derived it from some prompter's copy,—I feel assured that it is the poet's word. The same correction occurred, long ago, to myself: it occurred also to Mr. Collier, while he was editing the play; and (as appears from his note ad l.) he would have inserted it in the text, had not his better judgment been overpowered by a superstitious reverence for the folio.

But, if the Manuscript-corrector considered " *on*" to be an adverb (and we are uncertain how he understood it,—" *on*" and " *one*" being so often spelt alike), my conviction would still remain unshaken, that the recent editors, by printing " on," have greatly impaired the grandeur and the poetry of the passage. Steevens well observes; " The repeated strokes have less of solemnity than the single notice, as they take from the horror and awful silence here described as so propitious to the dreadful purposes of the king. Though the hour of *one* be not the natural midnight, it is yet the most solemn moment of the poetical one; and Shakespeare himself has chosen to introduce his Ghost in Hamlet,—

' The bell then beating *one*.' "

As to the " *contradiction*" which the recent editors object to in " the *midnight* bell sounding *one*," I can only say that, in such a passage, a poet may be forgiven for not expressing himself according to the exact matter of fact, when even prose-writers, from the earliest times to the present, occasionally employ very inaccurate language in speaking of the hours of darkness: *e. g.*;

" It happened that *betweene twelve and one a clocke at midnight*, there blew a mighty storme of winde against the house," &c. *The Famous History of Doctor Faustus*, sig. K 3, ed. 1648.

"We marched slowly on because of the carriages we had with us, and came to Freynstat about *one a clock in the night* perfectly undiscover'd." Defoe's *Memoirs of a Cavalier*, p. 119, first ed.

"Left Ostend in the steam-boat *at three o'clock in the night*." *Journal* by Cary, the translator of Dante,—*Memoir* of him by his Son, vol. ii. 254.

Act iv. sc. 1.
"Yet, I remember, when I was in France,
Young gentlemen would be as sad as night,
Only for wantonness."

"I doubt," says Malone, "whether our author had any authority for attributing this species of affectation to the French. He generally ascribes the manners of England to all other countries."

The French may or may not have been the inventors of this singular mark of gentility, which, it is well known, was once highly fashionable in England. But Nash, in one of his tracts, expressly mentions an assumed melancholy as one of the follies which "idle travellers" brought home from France. The passage is very curious. "What is there in Fraunce to be learnd more than in England, but falshood in fellowship, perfect slouenrie, to loue no man but for my pleasure, to sweare *Ah par la mort Dieu* when a mans hammes are scabd? For the idle Traueller (I meane not for the Souldiour), I have knowen some that haue continued there by the space of halfe a dozen yeare, and when they come [came] home, they haue hyd a little weerish leane face vnder a broad French hat, kept a terrible coyle with the dust in the streete in their long cloakes

of gray paper, and spoke English strangely. Nought else
haue they profited by their trauell, saue learnt to distin-
guish of the true Burdeaux grape, and knowe a cup of
neate Gascoygne wine from wine of Orleance; yea, and
peraduenture this also, to esteeme of the poxe as a pimple,
to weare a veluet patch on their face, *and walke melancholy with their armes folded.*" *The Vnfortvnate Traveller.
Or, The Life of Jacke Wilton*, 1594, sig. L 4.

Act v. sc. 2.

" This *unheard* sauciness, and boyish troops," &c.

So the old copies.

" The manuscript-corrector gives no countenance to
Theobald's proposal to read *unhair'd* for ' unheard;' and
that his attention was directed to the line, is evident from
the fact that he makes an emendation, though not of much
importance, in it; he reads :—

' This unheard sauciness *of* boyish troops.' "

Collier's *Notes and Emendations*, &c. p. 210.

Theobald did more than "*propose* to read *unhair'd*,"—
he fearlessly inserted it in the text; and all his successors,
excepting Mr. Collier, have retained it.

The Manuscript-corrector's alteration (made, I presume, because he had forgotten that *hair* and *hair'd* were
often spelt *hear* and *heard*,—*e. g.*;

" In face, in clothes, in speech, in eyes, in *heare*."
Harington's *Orlando Furioso*, B. xliii. st. 34.

" Franticke Ambition, Enuie, shagge-*heard* Lust."
Chapman's *Euthymniæ Raptus*, &c. 1609, sig. F.)

introduces a genitive case, where, there is every reason to believe, Shakespeare did not intend one to occur ;

> " *This* apish and unmannerly *approach,*
> *This* harness'd *masque,* and unadvised *revel,*
> *This* unhair'd *sauciness,* and boyish *troops,*
> The king doth smile at; and is well prepar'd
> To whip *this* dwarfish *war, these* pigmy *arms,*
> From out the circle of his territories."

Besides, we may well doubt if any writer would or could use " unheard sauciness" for " unheard-*of* sauciness."

" *Unhair'd* sauciness" is, of course, *unbearded* sauciness; and (as I remarked in a former publication) Faulconbridge now expresses *to* the Dauphin that contempt for him and his forces, with which in the preceding scene he had spoken *of* him to the King ;

> " shall a *beardless* boy,
> A cocker'd silken wanton, brave our fields ?" &c.

RICHARD II.

Act v. sc. 1.

"thou most beauteous *inn*,
Why should hard-favour'd *grief be lodg'd in thee,*
When triumph is become an ale-house guest?"

Compare Dante, in the *Vita Nuova;*

"O voi, che per la via d' Amor passate,
    Attendete, e guardate
      S' egli è dolore alcun quanto il mio graue:
    È prego sol ch' à vdir mi soffriate;
    È poi imaginate,
      S' io son *d'* ogni *dolore hostello* e chiaue."

P. 9, ed. 1576.

FIRST PART OF HENRY IV.

Act i. sc. 2.
> "Hear me, *Yedward*."

The commentators pass over "*Yedward*" without any remark.—It is a familiar corruption of "Edward," and, I believe, still retained in Cheshire and Lancashire.

Towards the end of the first act of Shadwell's *Lancashire Witches*, Clod, who speaks in the Lancashire dialect, uses "*Yedard*" for "Edward;"

"*Doubt.* Whose house is that?
Clod. Why, what a pox, where han yeow lived? why, yeow are strongers indeed! Why, 'tis Sir *Yedard* Hartfort's," &c.

Act iii. sc. 2.
> "rash *bavin* wits,
> Soon kindled, and soon burn'd."

The editors give no example of "*bavin*" used adjectively. The following passage affords one;

"Nay, M. Mamon, misinterpret not;
I onely burne the *bauen* heath of youth,
That cannot court the presence of faire time
With ought but with, What newes at court, sweet sir?"
Jacke Drums Entertainement, sig. A 3, ed. 1616.

Act iv. sc. 1.

"The quality and *hair* of our attempt
Brooks no division."

"In the quartos of 1598 and 1599, 'heire' [of the folio] was *haire*, the old mode of spelling *hair;* and this, the old corrector assures us, was the true word, the meaning of the speaker being (as suggested in note I), that the power he, and the other revolted lords could produce, was too small to allow of any division of it." Collier's *Notes and Emendations*, &c. p. 237.

That "*hair*" is "the true word," was probably never questioned by a single reader of the passage, with the exception of Boswell (who thought that "perhaps *hair* is put for *air*"), and of Mr. Knight (who inserts "air" in his text). That Mr. Collier is quite mistaken about "the meaning of the speaker," I have indisputably proved in *Remarks on Collier's and Knight's eds. of Shakespeare*, p. 108.

Act v. sc. 2.

"Sound all the lofty instruments of war,
And by that music let us all embrace;
For, heaven to earth, some of us never shall
A second time do such a courtesy."

"Warburton," writes Mr. Collier, "was of opinion that the poet meant that the odds were so great, that heaven might be wagered against earth, that many present would never embrace again. This is a mistake, according to the manuscript-corrector: Hotspur calls heaven and earth to witness to the improbability that some of those present would ever have an opportunity of regreeting each other:—

> "'*Fore* heaven *and* earth, some of us never shall
> A second time do such a courtesy.'"
>
> Notes and Emendations, &c. p. 239.

In the first place:—"'*Fore heaven*" is a sort of petty oath which belongs to familiar dialogue (as in *Othello*, act ii. sc. 3, "'*Fore heaven*, they have given me a rouse,"— "'*Fore heaven*, an excellent song"), and is therefore altogether at variance with the solemn tone of the present passage. In the second place:—if any one should urge that "the expression substituted by the Manuscript-corrector is not '*Fore heaven*,' but '*Fore heaven* and earth'" (a very unusual expression indeed), and that "we find something similar in *The Tempest*, act iv. sc. 1,

> '*afore heaven*
> I ratify this my rich gift,'"—

my answer is, that, even supposing "'*Fore heaven and earth*" to be a formula of attestation not inadmissible in a passage of the utmost seriousness, still we have what amounts almost to positive proof that Shakespeare did not employ it *here;* because the word "For,"—which the Manuscript-corrector converts into "'*Fore*,"—seems indispensably necessary to *introduce the reason why they should all embrace* on that occasion,—

> " *Sound all the lofty instruments of war,*
> *And by that music let us all embrace;*
> FOR," &c.

Act v. sc. 3.

"*Hot.* The king hath many *marching* in his coats."

" This is intelligible, and does not positively require change; but the old corrector substitutes a word for ' marching' (the forces, at this time, were fighting, not marching), which seems much better adapted to the place :—

' The king hath many *masking* in his coats.' "

Collier's *Notes and Emendations,* &c. p. 240.

Surely, the Manuscript-corrector was perfectly right when he made this alteration. In *Tamburlaine, Part First,* act v. sc. 2, a line used to stand thus,—

" And *march* in cottages of strowed reeds,"—

till, in my edition of Marlowe's *Works,* i. 99, I altered " *march*" to " mask."

SECOND PART OF HENRY IV.

Act ii. sc. 3.

"The time was, father, that you broke your word,
When you were more *endear'd* to it than now."

Here "*endear'd*" is equivalent to—engaged, bound. The word is used much in the same sense by Day;

"You did *indeare* him to society
Of carelesse wantons," &c.
Law-Trickes, 1608, sig. H 2.

Act ii. sc. 3.

"it [*i. e.* his honour] *stuck* upon him, as the sun
In the grey vault of heaven."

To modern readers there is perhaps something coarse in this expression; but it was not so to those of Shakespeare's days;

"While Lucifer fore-shewes Auroras springs,
And Arctos *stickes* aboue the earth vnmou'd," &c.
Chapman's *Byrons Tragedie*, sig. N 4, ed. 1608.

"No black-eyed star must *sticke* in vertues spheare."
Dekker's *Satiromastix*, 1602, sig L 2.

Act ii. sc. 4.

"Then, death, rock me asleep, abridge my *doleful days!*
Why then, let grievous, ghastly, gaping wounds
Untwine *the sisters three!* Come, *Atropos*, I say!"

It can hardly be doubted, I think, that, in this rant of Pistol, Shakespeare had an eye to the following passage of *Buckingham's Complaynt,* written by Sackville;

"But what may boote to stay *the Sisters three,*
When *Atropos* perforce will cut the thred?
The *dolefull day* was come, when you might see
Northampton fielde with armed men orespred," &c.
St. 6 (*Mirrour for Magistrates*).

Act v. sc. 3.

"a dish of *carraways.*"

Here "*carraways*" is rightly explained by Warburton (though his explanation has been ignorantly questioned), "a comfit or confection so called in our author's time,"—the said carraways being made, of course, with carraway seeds.

In Shadwell's *Woman-Captain,* carraway-comfits are mentioned as no longer fit to appear at fashionable tables; "the fruit, crab-apples, sweetings and horse-plumbs; and for *confections,* a few *carraways* in a small sawcer, as if his worship's house had been a lowsie inn." *Works,* iii. 350.

SECOND PART OF HENRY VI.

Act i. sc. 3.

" 1 *Pet.* My masters, let's stand close: my lord Protector will come this way by and by, and then we may deliver our supplications *in the quill.*"

Much has been written about "*in the quill.*" Mr. Hunter (*New Illustr. of Shakespeare,* ii. 66) says that "' quill' means here the narrow passage through which the Protector was to pass;" and he infers this meaning from the following lines in Sylvester's *Du Bartas* (*The Ark,* p. 114, ed. 1641);

" And th' endlesse, thin ayre (which by secret *quils*
Had lost it selfe within the winds-but hils," &c.

But if we turn to the original French, it will be seen that no light is thrown on "*quill*" in Shakespeare by "*quils*" in Sylvester, who used the word merely because he was translating literally;

" Et puis l'air infini, qui par secrets *tuyaux,*
Rare, c'estoit perdu dans les sombres caueaux
Des monts butes des vents," &c.

In a later part of the same work (*The Tropheis,* p. 201) Sylvester has,

" Anon, like Cedron, through a straighter *quill*
Thou strainest out a little brook or rill;"

the original of which is,

> " or dans un sec *tuyau*
> Pousses, comme Cedron, vn petit filet d'eau."

(" *Tuyau.* A pipe, *quill,* cane, reed, canell." Cotgrave's *Dict.*)

" The several petitioners," says Mr. Collier, " were to deliver their supplications to Suffolk in succession, one after another, and ' the quill' ought, indisputably, to be *sequel,* used ignorantly for sequence." *Notes and Emendations,* &c. p. 280.

But why should Peter, whose language is elsewhere correct enough, "use" a word "ignorantly" on this one occasion? Besides, when a dramatist puts a wrong word into the mouth of a comic character, there is always something ludicrous, or inclining to the ludicrous, in the mistake of the speaker: according to the Manuscript-corrector's alteration, there is nothing of the kind here.

Read "in the *quoil*"=*coil* (i.e. *the stir* which will take place when the Protector comes).

THIRD PART OF HENRY VI.

Act ii. sc. 5.
" *Fath. These arms of mine* shall be thy winding-sheet;
My heart, sweet boy, *shall be thy sepulchre,*
* * * * * * * *
And so obsequious will thy father be,
Men, for the loss of thee, having no more,
As Priam was for all his valiant sons."

When Shakespeare wrote the first two lines (to which there is nothing parallel in *The True Tragedie of Richard Duke of Yorke*), he was thinking, it would seem, of Marlowe's *Jew of Malta*, where the Governor, on seeing the dead body of his son, exclaims,—

" What sight is this ? my Lodowick [Lodovico] slain !
These arms of mine shall be thy sepulchre."
Marlowe's *Works*, i. 289, ed. Dyce.

In the last line but one, the misprint " *Men*" was altered by Rowe to " Sad," which Malone and Mr. Knight adopted. Steevens conjectured " Man," and Mr. Collier inserted it in his text.

" The word ' Men' is merely the printer's mistake, who carelessly began the line with *M* instead of *E* :—

' *E'en* for the loss of thee,' &c.

There can be little objection to receive this trifling, but

effectual, emendation at the hands of the old corrector."
Collier's *Notes and Emendations*, &c. p. 293.

Mr. Collier appears not to be aware that in my *Remarks*, &c., published in 1844, I said, " Surely ' *Men*' must be a misprint for ' E'en.'" p. 133.

RICHARD III.

Act i. sc. 2.
"*Anne.* Set down, set down your honourable load."

Here Shakespeare had in his recollection a line at the commencement of a scene in the Sec. Part of *The Troublesome Raigne of King John;*

"*Set downe, set downe* the *loade* not worth your paine."
Sig. K 4, ed. 1622.

Act i. sc. 4.
" false, *fleeting*, perjur'd Clarence."

The word "*fleeting,*" applied to a *person*, is of very rare occurrence (Steevens, I presume, could call to mind no instance of it, for he illustrates the present line by "the *fleeting* moon" from *Antony and Cleopatra*). Sir John Harington, in his *Orlando Furioso*, has;

" But Griffin (though he came not for this end,
For praise and bravery at tilt to run,
But came to find his *fleeting* female friend)," &c.
B. xvii. st. 18.

Act iii. sc. 4.
" And this is Edward's wife, that monstrous witch,
Consorted with that *harlot, strumpet* Shore,
That by their witchcraft thus have marked me."

So Malone, Mr. Collier, and Mr. Knight, with an erroneous punctuation in the second line, which ought to stand,—

"Consorted with that *harlot strumpet* Shore,"—

"*harlot*" being here an adjective. Compare;

"O *harlot whore*, why should I stay my hands?
* * * * * * * *
Locrinus now (quoth she) had not thus dide,
If such an *harlot whore* he had not tooke."
A Mirour for Magistrates, &c. p. 34, ed. 1610.

Act v. sc. 3.
"I *died for hope*, ere I could lend thee aid."

The reading, "*died for hope*," has been questioned: but (however we are to understand it) the following passage in Greene's *James the Fourth* seems to determine that it is right;

"'Twixt love and fear continual are the wars.
The one assures me of my Ida's love,
The other moves me for my murder'd queen.
Thus find I grief of that whereon I joy,
And doubt in greatest hope, and death in weal.
Alas, what hell may be compar'd with mine,
Since in extremes my comforts do consist!
War then will cease, when dead ones are reviv'd;
Some then will yield, when I am *dead for hope*."
Works, ii. 149, ed. Dyce.

HENRY VIII.

Act ii. sc. 2.
"*Enter* Wolsey *and* Campeius."

Shakespeare is not the only great poet that has introduced Campeius. In the *Orlando Furioso*, c. xlvi. st. 11, Lorenzo Campeggi figures among the illustrious persons who congratulate Ariosto on the completion of his labours.

Act iii. sc. 2.
" I have ventur'd,
Like little wanton boys that swim on bladders,
This many summers in *a sea of glory*," &c.

In Fairfax's *Tasso*, B. ii. st. 68, is,—

" The *sea of glorie* hath no bankes assignde,"—

a metaphor not in the original. That celebrated translation* appeared in 1600. Shakespeare's *Henry VIII.*, there seems to be no doubt, was produced at a later date.

* It has been praised somewhat beyond its merits by critics who knew very little about the original. That Fairfax possessed considerable power as a poet, is not to be denied: but unfortunately, instead of being content to *translate* Tasso, he is *continually introducing allusions and similes of his own invention*, and frequently in the worst possible taste; for instance, at p. 186, ed. 1600;

" This said, that narrow entrance past the knight,
(*So creepes a camell through a needles eie*)," &c. ! ! !

Often, too, he falls into the most outrageous tautology: there are hundreds of passages like the following;

> " With publike praier, zeale, and faith deuout,
> The *aide, assistance, and the helpe* obtaine
> Of all the blessed of the heau'nly rout,
> With whose support you conquest sure may gaine." p. 195.
> (" Sia dal cielo il principio: invoca innanti,
> Nelle preghiere pubbliche e devote,
> La milizia degli Angioli e de' Santi,
> Che ne impetri vittoria ella che puote.")

> "Tomorrow is a day of paines and war,
> This *of repose, of quiet, peace and rest;*
> Goe, take your ease *this euening and this night,*" &c. p. 198.
> (" Quel fia giorno di guerra e di sudore;
> Questo sia d' apparecchio e di quiete:
> Dunque ciascun vada al riposo," &c.)

> " From their strong foes vpon them following
> To [Thou] maist them *keepe, preserue, saue and defend.*" p. 216.
> (" Se stuol nemico seguitando viene,
> Lui risospingi, e lor salva e defendi.")

> " This said, he fled *through skies, through cloudes, and aire."* p. 220.
> (" Ciò disse; e poi n' andò per l' aria a volo.")

To haste or carelessness perhaps we must attribute such a mistake as this;

> " He turnd about, and to good Sigiere spake,
> Who bare *his greatest sheild* and mightie bow,
> *That sure and trustie target let me take,*
> Impenetrable is that sheild I know," &c. p. 206.
> (" Onde rivolto, dice al buon Sigiero,
> Che gli portava *un altro scudo* e l' arco:
> Ora mi porgi, o fedel mio scudiero,
> *Cotesto meno assai gravoso incarco,*" &c.)

It is by exchanging his *large* shield for a *lesser* shield that Godfrey exposes himself to the shafts of Clorinda, who forthwith wounds him.

TROILUS AND CRESSIDA.

Act i. sc. 3.

An.   " the thing of courage,
As rous'd with rage, with rage doth sympathize,
And, with an accent tun'd in self-same key,
Retires to chiding fortune."

The modern editors give (with Pope) " Returns." Hanmer read " Replies ;" and so the Manuscript-corrector of the folio, 1632.

Did not Shakespeare write " *Retorts* to chiding fortune ?"

Act iii. sc. 2.

" The falcon *as* the tercel, for all the ducks i' the river."

Mr. Collier's note on this passage is ; " The meaning seems to be, that the 'falcon,' or female hawk, is as good as the 'tercel,' the male hawk."—Tyrwhitt unnecessarily proposed to read " *at* the tercel."

Monck Mason's explanation, " I will back the falcon against the tiercel—I will wager that the falcon is equal to the tiercel," is proved to be the right one by a passage in Fletcher's *Love's Pilgrimage*, when Diego and Incubo are parting different ways in search of Leocadia. Mason has cited only a portion of that passage : I subjoin it entire ;

"*Inc.* Best to divide.

Diego. I'll this way.

Inc. And I this.

Diego. I, *as you,* find him for a real!

Inc. 'Tis done.

Diego. My course is now directly to some pie-house;
I know the pages' compass.

Inc. I think rather
The smock-side o' the town the surer harbour
At his years to put in.

Diego. If I do find
The hungry haunt, I take him by the teeth now.

Inc. I by the tail; yet I *as you.*

Diego. No more. [*Exeunt severally.*"
Act v. sc. 1.

ROMEO AND JULIET.

Act ii. sc. 1.
" Young *Abraham* Cupid, he that shot so trim," &c.

Upton altered " *Abraham*" to " Adam," understanding the allusion to be to the celebrated archer *Adam* Bell; and, since Upton's time, the alteration has been adopted by all editors, except Mr. Knight, who retains "*Abraham*," which he explains to mean " the cheat—the 'Abraham man'—of our old statutes."

That Shakespeare here had an eye to the ballad of *King Cophetua and the Beggar Maid*, is certain;

> " The blinded boy *that shootes so trim*
> From heaven down did *hie*,
> He drew a dart, and shot at him
> In place where he did lye."

But this stanza contains nothing to countenance in the slightest degree the reading " *Adam* Cupid."

In *Soliman and Perseda*, 1599, we find,—

> " Where is the eldest sonne of Pryam,
> That *abraham*-coloured Troion? dead."
>
> Sig. H 3.

in Middleton's *Blurt, Master Constable*, 1602,—

> " A goodlie, long, thicke, *Abram*-colour'd beard."
>
> Sig. D.

and in our author's *Coriolanus,* act ii. sc. 3, according to the first three folios, " not that our heads are some browne, some blacke, som *Abram ;*" there being hardly any reason to doubt that in these passages " *abraham*" (or " *Abram*") is a corruption of " *abron,*" which our early writers frequently employ for " *auburn.*" Is, then, the right reading in the present line,—

" Young *abram* [or *auburn*] Cupid," &c.,

Shakespeare having used " *abram*" for " auburn-*haired,*" as the author of *Soliman and Perseda* has used " *abraham*-colour'd Troion" for " Trojan with auburn-coloured *hair?*" Every body familiar with the Italian poets knows that they term Cupid, as well as Apollo, " Il bióndo Dio:" and W. Thomas, in his *Principal Rules of the Italian Grammer,* &c., gives; " *Biondo,* the *aberne* [i. e. *auburn*] colour, that is betwene white and yelow." Sig. E 2, ed. 1567. In *The Two Gentlemen of Verona,* act iv. sc. 4, " *auburn*" means yellowish,—

" Her hair is *auburn,* mine is perfect yellow."

Act ii. sc. 2.

" at lovers' perjuries,
They say, Jove laughs."

Malone (who would not allow that Shakespeare could read Ovid) observes that he might " have caught this" from Greene's *Metamorphosis.* Yes; and he might have found it in Italian;

"Quel che si fa per ben Dio non aggrava,
Anzi ride el spergiuro de gli amanti."
　　　Bojardo,—*Orlando Innam.* lib. 1. c. xxii. st. 42.

Act iii. sc. 2.

"Spread thy close curtain, love-performing night,
That *run-aways* eyes may wink, and Romeo
Leap to these arms, untalk'd of, and unseen!"

"The line of Juliet's speech, as usually printed,

'That *run-away's* eyes may wink,' &c.

has always been a stumbling-block, and perhaps no emendation can be declared perfectly satisfactory. The change proposed by the corrector of the folio, 1632, at all events makes very clear sense out of the passage, although it may still remain a question, whether that sense be the sense of the poet? another subsidiary question will be, how so elaborate a misprint could have been made out of so simple and common a word? He gives . . . 'That *enemies*' eyes may wink.' . . . In the margin of the folio, 1632, *enemies* is spelt *enimyes;* but the letters are, perhaps, too few to have been mistaken for *run-awaies*. At the same time it seems extremely natural that Juliet should wish the eyes of *enemies* to be closed," &c. Collier's *Notes and Emendations,* &c. p. 381.

Both Mr. Collier and Mr. Knight, in their editions of *Shakespeare,* adopted the villanous conjecture of Zachary Jackson,—" That, *unawares,* eyes may wink:" and other conjectures have more recently been offered by myself and others, all perhaps bad enough, but certainly quite as good as the Manuscript-corrector's "*enemies*'."

The spelling of the first folio is "run-awayes," not, as Mr. Collier seems to suppose, "*run-awaies.*"

I now venture to submit another conjecture to the reader;—

"That *roving* eyes may wink," &c.

a conjecture founded on the supposition that the word "*roving*" having been written (and written rather illegibly) "*roauinge*" (Fairfax, in his *Tasso*, B. iv. st. 87, has,

"At some her gazing glances *roauing* flew"),

the compositor metamorphosed it into "run-awayes."

Act iv. sc. 4.

"*Cap.* Come stir, stir, stir! the second cock hath crow'd,
The curfew-bell hath rung, 'tis three o'clock:—
Look to the bak'd meats, good Angelica;
Spare not for cost.
 Nurse.   Go, go, you *cot-quean*, go.
Get you to bed: 'faith, you'll be sick tomorrow
For this night's watching.
 Cap. No, not a whit. What! I have watch'd ere now
All night for lesser cause, and ne'er been sick.
 La. Cap. Ay, you have been a mouse-hunt in your time," &c.

"A *cot-quean*," says Mr. Hunter, "is the wife of a faithless husband, and not, as Johnson, who knew little of the language of Shakespeare's time, explains it, 'a man who busies himself about kitchen affairs.' It occurs twice in Golding's translation of the story of Tereus. The Nurse is speaking to Lady Capulet, and the word calls forth all the conversation which follows about jealousy. Authorities for this being the true sense might be produced in abundance." *New Illustr. of Shakespeare,* ii. 138.

But Golding, in the passage to which Mr. Hunter refers, has *cuc-queane,* which is a distinct word from *cot-quean,* though they are sometimes confounded by early writers,—a *cuc-quean* (*cuck-quean,* or *cock-quean*) meaning a she-cuckold; a *cot-quean,* a man who busies himself too much in women's affairs. In Fletcher's *Love's Cure,* act ii. sc. 2, Bobadilla says to Lucio (who has been brought up as a girl), "*Diablo!* what should you do in the kitchen? cannot the cooks lick their fingers, without your overseeing? nor the maids make pottage, except your dog's head be in the pot? Don Lucio? Don *Quot-quean,* Don Spinster! wear a petticoat still, and put on your smock a' Monday; I will have a baby o' clouts made for it, like a great girl;"—where "*Quot-quean*" is a corrupt form of "*Cot-quean.*" Even in Addison's days the word *cot-quean* was still used to signify one who is too busy in meddling with women's affairs: see the letter of an imaginary lady in *The Spectator,* No. 482.—Mr. Hunter's notion, that "the Nurse is speaking to *Lady* Capulet," is, I think, sufficiently disproved by the context.

Act v. sc. 1.

" If I may trust the flattering *eye* of sleep,
My dreams presage some joyful news at hand."

So Malone, following the valuable quarto of 1597. The meaning (about which he and some other commentators make such a pother) is, in vulgar prose,—*If I may trust the visions with which my eye flattered me during sleep.*

Both Mr. Collier and Mr. Knight give, with the quarto of 1599, the later quartos, and the folios, "the flattering *truth* of sleep:" Mr. Collier, however, makes no attempt to explain that reading; neither does Mr. Knight, who merely observes, " It is not difficult to see the growth of that philosophical spirit in Shakespeare which suggested the substitution of the word ' truth,' which opens to the mind a deep volume of metaphysical inquiry,"—intimating perhaps that it would require a whole volume to make plain to us what Shakespeare meant by the word " truth."

The *Notes and Emendations*, &c. furnish us with a new reading. " Sleep," says Mr. Collier, " is often resembled to death, and death to sleep; and when Romeo observes, as the correction in the folio, 1632, warrants us in giving the passage,—

' If I may trust the flattering *death* of sleep,'

he calls it ' the flattering death of sleep' on account of the dream of joyful news from which he had awaked: during this ' flattering death of sleep,' he had dreamed of Juliet, and of her revival of him by the warmth of her kisses." p. 384.

Now, I have not forgotten how our early writers characterise Sleep,—for instance, I recollect that Sleep is called by Sackville " cousin of Death" and "a living death," and by Daniel, " brother to Death;" but I remember nothing in the whole range of poetry which bears any resemblance to such a combination of words as " *the flattering death of sleep;*" and, though I may lay myself open to the charge of presumption, I unhesitatingly assert, not only that the expression never could have come from Shakespeare's pen, but that it is akin to nonsense.

Act v. sc. 1.

"[*Rom.*] The world is not thy friend, nor the world's law:
The world affords no law to make thee rich;
Then, be not poor, but break it, and *take this.*
Ap. My poverty, but not my will, consents.
Rom. I *pay* thy poverty, and not thy will."

A writer in *The Westminster Review,* vol. xliv. p. 61, says that "Mr. Knight [in the last line of the above passage] very properly restores the reading of the second 4to and the first folio, ' pray:' the relation here is between Romeo's *earnestly repeated prayer* and the apothecary's *consent:* the moment for *paying* him is not yet arrived." But what does the writer understand by the concluding words of Romeo's preceding speech, "take *this?*" can he doubt that "*this*" means the gold which Romeo holds in his hand, ready to pay the Apothecary?

Act v. sc. 3.
"*Par.* I do defy thy *conjurations.*"

Both Mr. Knight and Mr. Collier having rejected the reading "*conjurations*" for the misprint " commiseration," and Mr. Collier having observed that " the sense of *conjurations* is not clear," I adduced a passage from an early drama, where "*conjuration*" signifies *earnest entreaty* (see *Remarks,* &c. p. 176). It may not be useless to notice here, that the word occurs in the same sense in a once-admired modern novel: " the arguments, or rather the *conjurations,* of which I have made use," &c. Mrs. Sheridan's *Sidney Bidulph,* vol. v. p. 74.

JULIUS CÆSAR.

Act iv. sc. 3.

" The enemy, marching along by them,
By them shall make a fuller number up,
Come on refresh'd, new-*added*, and encourag'd."

" The corrector of the folio, 1632, implies by his proposed change, that 'new-added' is merely a repetition of what is said in the preceding line—' by them shall make a fuller number up'—and he inserts a word instead of ' added,' which is not only more forcible, but more appropriate, and which we may very fairly suppose had been misheard by the scribe :—

' By them shall make a fuller number up,
Come on refresh'd, new-*hearted*, and encourag'd.'

The error might be occasioned by the then broad pronunciation of ' added' having been mistaken for *hearted*." Collier's *Notes and Emendations*, &c. p. 402.

I can hardly think that Mr. Collier is serious in the concluding sentence.

Here the Manuscript-corrector does away with one " repetition," only to introduce another: for what is the difference between " *hearted*" and " encourag'd ?"

Read,—

" Come on refresh'd, new-*aided*, and encourag'd."

Act v. sc. 1.

"I draw a sword against conspirators;
When think you that the sword goes up again?—
Never, till Cæsar's three and twenty wounds
Be well aveng'd; or till another Cæsar
Have added slaughter to the *sword* of *traitors*."

"Steevens," says Mr. Collier, "subjoined what he considered a parallel passage from 'King John,' act ii. sc. 2:—

'Or add a royal number to the dead,
With slaughter coupled to the name of kings.'

There is certainly some resemblance, but it is stronger when the quotation from 'Julius Cæsar' is printed as the old corrector advises:—

'or till another Cæsar
Have added slaughter to the *word* of *traitor*.'

Octavius terms Brutus a traitor, and challenges him to add slaughter to the *word*, in the same way that slaughter in 'King John' was to be coupled 'to the name of kings.' This emendation seems plausible, though we may not be disposed to insist upon it." *Notes and Emendations*, &c. p. 402.

The Manuscript-corrector's alteration (to say nothing of its tameness) is a most unnecessary one. Surely, Octavius means;—"or till you, traitors, have added the crime of slaying me (another Cæsar) to that of having murdered Julius."

MACBETH.

Act i. sc. 3.
> " As thick as *tale*,
> Came post with post."

Mr. Collier (*Notes and Emendations*, &c. p. 406) informs us that the Manuscript-corrector of the folio, 1632, has left the word "tale" unaltered.

In my *Remarks on Collier's and Knight's eds. of Shakespeare*, p. 188, I declared myself "*strongly inclined* to believe that 'hail' is the right reading :" I now entertain no doubt that it is so ; because I am convinced that such an expression as "thick as *tale*" was never employed by any writer whatsoever ; while, on the contrary, "thick as hail" is of common occurrence ;

> " Curse, ban, and breath out damned orisons,
> *As thicke as haile-stones* for[e] the springs approach."
> > *First Part of The Troublesome Raigne of King John*,
> > sig. F 4, ed. 1622.

> " The English archers shoot *as thick as haile*."
> > Harington's *Orlando Furioso*, B. xvi. st. 51.

> " Rayning down bullets from a stormy cloud,
> *As thick as hail*, upon their armies proud."
> > Sylvester's *Du Bartas,—Fourth Day of First Week*,
> > p. 38, ed. 1641.

> " More *thick* they fall *then haile*," &c.
> > *A Herrings Tayle*, &c. 1598, sig. C 2.

"*Darts thick as haile* their backs behinde did smite."
Niccols's *King Arthur,—A Winter Night's Vision*, &c.
(Contin. of *A Mir. for Mag.*), 1610, p. 583.

Act i. sc. 3.
" Come what come may,
Time and the hour runs through the roughest day "

The commentators have given several examples of this expression from English authors. It is not unfrequent in Italian;

" Ma perch' e' fugge *il tempo, e così l' ora,*
La nostra storia ci convien seguire."
Pulci,—*Morg. Mag.* c. xv. last stanza.

"Ferminsi in un momento *il tempo e l' ore.*"
Michelagnolo,—*Son.* xix.

" Aspettar vuol ch' occasion gli dia,
Come dar gli potrebbe, *il tempo e l' hora.*"
Dolce,—*Prime Imprese del Conte Orlando,*
c. xvii. p. 145, ed. 1572.

Act i. sc. 4.
" Thou art so far before,
That swiftest *wing* of recompense is slow
To overtake thee."

The second folio has "*wine* of recompense,"—which the Manuscript-corrector of that folio alters to "*wind* of recompense;" and Mr. Collier says, " This may, or may not, have been the line as it came from the poet's pen:

at all events, and for some unexplained reason, a person writing soon after 1632 seems to have preferred *wind* to 'wing,' when either would answer the purpose." *Notes and Emendations,* &c. p. 407.

I cannot be persuaded that " either reading would answer the purpose:" I think that " wing" is decidedly right,—that " *wind*" is one of the worst emendations in Mr. Collier's volume.

Act i. sc. 5.
" *the golden round,*
Which fate and metaphysical aid doth seem
To have thee crown'd withal."

The words which Shakespeare here applies to *a diadem* had been previously applied to *a ring* by Abraham Fraunce ;

" Wedding ring, farewell! shee's gone, whose yuory finger
Should haue been thy grace : full well did I cause to be grauen
In thy *golden round* those words as true as a Gospell,
Loue is a bitter-sweete, fit woords for bitter Alexis."
Sec. Part of The Countesse of Pembrokes Yuychurch,
1591, sig. K 4.*

---

* Perhaps in Milton (who was a careful reader of many poets now long forgotten) we may trace some slight obligations to Fraunce's hexameters;

" I fled, and cried out *Death !*
Hell trembled at the hideous name, and sigh'd
From all her caves, and *back resounded Death.*"
Par. Lost, b. ii. 787.

" Death, sayd euery man : Death, death with an eccho rebounded."
The Countess of Pembrokes Emanuel, 1591, sig. c 2.

Act i. sc. 6.
"Buttress nor *coigne* of vantage."
The editors are at a loss for an example of *coigne* in

"Darkness must overshadow all his bounds,
Palpable darkness, and blot out three days."
Par. Lost, b. xii. 187.
"There shall fogs and mystes and smokes and *palpable horror*
Wring out teares from her eyes," &c.
First Part of the Countess of Pembrokes *Yuychurch*,
1591, sig. B 2.

I take this opportunity of pointing out a few of Milton's *recollections* of various writers, which his editors have failed to notice:—

1.   "The imperial *ensign;* which, full high advanc'd,
      Shone *like a meteor* streaming to the wind," &c.
Par. Lost, b. i. 536.
"In Sion towres hangs his victorious *flagge*,
Blowing defiance this way; and it showes
Like a red meteor in the troubled aire," &c.
Heywood's *Four Prentices of London*, sig. G, ed. 1615.

2.   "*Behold a wonder!* They but now," &c.   *Par. Lost.* b. i. 777.
      "and yet (*behold a wonder*)," &c.
Harington's *Orlando Furioso*, b. i. st. 22.

3.   "In darkness, and *with dangers compass'd round*."
Par. Lost, b. vii. 27.
"But being now *with danger compast round*."
Harington's *Orlando Furioso*, b. i. st. 50.

4.   "Grace was in all her steps."   *Par. Lost*, b. viii. 488.
"Nè senza somma grazia un passo muove."
Ariosto, *Orlando Fur.* c. xlvi. st. 92.

5.   "To behold the wandering *moon*,
      Riding near her highest *noon*."   *Il Penseroso*.
"Now the goodly *moone*
Was in the full, and at her nighted *noone*."
Drayton's *Man in the Moone*,—*Poems*, p. 476, fol.

any other writer than Shakespeare. It is certainly a word of rare occurrence :—

> " And Cape of Hope, last *coign* of Africa."
> Sylvester's *Du Bartas,—The Colonies*,
> p. 129, ed. 1641.

(The original has " *angle* dernier d'Afrique.")

Act i. sc. 7.

> " *Macb.* Pr'ythee, peace.
> I dare do all that may become a man ;
> Who dares do more is none.
> *Lady M.* What *beast* was't, then,
> That made you break this enterprize to me ?
> When you durst do it, then you were a man," &c.

" Surely," says Mr. Collier, " it reads like a gross vulgarism for Lady Macbeth thus to ask, ' What beast made him divulge the enterprize to her ?' but she means nothing

---

6.   " Find out *some uncouth cell.*"   *L'Allegro.*
       " Upon our plaines, or in *some uncouth cell.*"
           Wither and Browne's *Shepheards Pipe (The Seventh Eglogue)*, sig. K 8, ed. 1620.

7   " O *nightingale*, that on yon bloomy *spray*
       Warblest at eve," &c.
                                    Sonnet i.
       " Thence thirty steps, amid the leafie *sprayes*
       Another *nightingale* repeats her layes."
           Sylvester's *Du Bartas,—Fifth Day of First Week*,
               p. 44, ed. 1641.

8.   " *Of which all Europe rings* from side to side."
                                      Sonnet xxii.
       " And *of the which all Europe now doth ring.*"
           Harington's *Orlando Furioso*, b. xlvi. st. 55.

of the kind: she alludes to Macbeth's former vaunt that he was eager for the deed, and yet could not now 'screw his courage' to the point, when time and place had, as it were, 'made themselves' for its execution: this she calls [according to the Manuscript-corrector of the folio, 1632] a mere *boast* on his part:—

> 'What *boast* was't, then,
> That made you break this enterprize to me?'

she charges him with being a vain braggart, first to profess to be ready to murder Duncan, and afterwards, from fear, to relinquish it. That this emendation might be guessed by a person who carefully read the text, without attention to the conventional mode of giving and understanding these words, we have this proof—that it was communicated to the editor of the present volume, six months ago, by an extremely intelligent gentleman, whose name we have no authority to give, but who dated from Aberdeen, and who had not the slightest knowledge that *boast*, for 'beast,' was the manuscript reading in the folio, 1632. It is very possible, therefore, that the old corrector of the folio, 1632, arrived at his conclusion upon the point by the same process: on the other hand, it is impossible to deny that he may have had some authority, printed,* written, or oral, for the proposed change; and it is quite certain that people have been in the habit of reading 'Macbeth' for the last 200 years, some of them for the express purpose of detecting blunders in the text, and yet, as far as can be ascertained, have never once hit upon this improvement, so trifling as regards typography, but

* I cannot conceive what *printed* authority Mr. Collier alludes to. Does he suppose that *Macbeth* appeared in print before it was included in the folio of 1623?

so valuable as respects the meaning of Shakespeare." *Notes and Emendations,* &c. p. 408.

For a moment, after first reading this emendation, I thought it a very happy one. On reflection, it appears to me very questionable.

An accomplished critic * has remarked on it as follows. "Here Mr. Collier reasons, as it appears to us, without sufficient reference to the context of the passage, and its place in the scene. The expression immediately preceding, and eliciting, Lady Macbeth's reproach, is that in which Macbeth declares that he dares do all that may become *a man,* and that who dares do more *is none.* She instantly takes up that expression. If not an affair in which *a man* may engage, what *beast* was it, then, in himself or others, that made him break this enterprise to her? The force of the passage lies in that contrasted word, and its meaning is lost by the proposed substitution." *The Examiner,* Jan. 29, 1853.

Mr. Collier (as we have just seen) speaks of "Macbeth's *former vaunt* that he *was eager for* the deed," and, in the Preface to his volume, p. xix., of Macbeth having "previously *vaunted his determination to murder Duncan.*" But where is the copy of the play which contains any thing of the sort? In the preceding scenes, according to the received text, the language of Macbeth, when talking to his wife about the murder, is as far removed from *vaunting* as it possibly can be.

Nor is the emendation of the Manuscript-corrector unobjectionable on the score of phraseology. A "*boast making* one *break* an enterprise to another" is hardly in the style of an experienced writer.

Be it also observed, that in *Antony and Cleopatra,*

* Mr. John Forster.

act i. sc. 5, the Manuscript-corrector has substituted " boastfully" for " *beastly*," to the destruction of the meaning evidently intended by the poet.

Act ii. sc. 2.
" The multitudinous seas incarnardine,
Making the green one, red."

To the passages cited here by the commentators, add—

" And, dronke with bloud, *from blue*
The sea take blushing hue;
As iuice of Tyrian shell,
When clarified well,
To wolle of finest fields
A purple glosse it yeeldes."
The Tragedie of Antonie, 1595, (by the Countess of Pembroke, from the French,) sig. F 8.

Act ii. sc. 4.
" A falcon, *towering* in her pride of place."

On " towering" the commentators have no remark, perhaps not being aware that it is a term of falconry. Donne, addressing Sir Henry Goodyere, and speaking of his hawk, says;

" Which when herselfe she lessens in the aire,
You then first say, that high enough she *toures.*"
Poems, p. 73, ed. 1633.

Turberville tells us; " Shee [the hobby] is of the

number of those Hawkes that are hie flying and *towre Hawks.*" *Booke of Falconrie,* p. 53, ed. 1611.

Act iii. sc. 3.
" and *near* approaches
The subject of our watch."

The Manuscript-corrector of the folio, 1632, " puts 'here' in his margin [for '*near*']; either may be right." Collier's *Notes and Emendations,* &c. p. 411.

If Mr. Collier had carefully considered the context, he would have perceived that "here" cannot be right:—

" 1 *Mur.* Then stand with us.
The west yet glimmers with some streaks of day:
Now spurs the lated traveller apace,
To gain the timely inn; and *near* approaches
The subject of our watch.
3 *Mur.* Hark! I hear horses.
Ban. [*within.*] Give us a light there, ho!
2 *Mur.* *Then it is he,*" &c.

The First Murderer knew, from the coming on of night, that Banquo was *not far off;* but, before hearing the tread of horses and the voice of Banquo, he could not know that the victim was absolutely *close at hand.*

Act iii. sc. 4.
" If trembling I *inhabit*, then protest me
The baby of a girl."

For this very doubtful reading of the old copies, the Manuscript-corrector of the folio, 1632, substitutes,

"If trembling I *exhibit*, then protest me," &c.

(*i. e.* If I exhibit trembling);—an alteration, which Mr. Collier allows to be "too prosaic" (*Notes and Emendations,* &c. p. 412), and which, in fact, is all but ludicrous.

Act iii. sc. 5.
" Get you gone,
And at the pit of *Acheron*
Meet me i' the morning."

It is not a little amusing to read the notes on "*Acheron*," and to find Malone almost persuaded by a Mr. Plumptre that Shakespeare was thinking here of "Ekron" in Scripture.* Did these matter-of-fact commentators suppose that Shakespeare himself, had they been able to call him up from the dead, could have told them "all about it?" Not he;—no more than Fairfax, who, in his translation of the *Gerusalemme* (published before *Macbeth* was produced), has made Ismeno frequent "the shores of *Acheron*," without any warrant from Tasso;

" A Christian once, Macon he now adores,
Nor could he quite his wonted faith forsake,
But in his wicked arts both oft implores
Helpe from the Lord and aide from Pluto blake;
He, from deepe caues by Acherons darke shores
(Where circles vaine and spels he vs'd to make),

---

* I understand that in *Macbeth*, as it is now acted at the Princess's Theatre, there is a *perfectly correct* representation of " *the pit of Acheron.*"

T' aduise his king in these extremes is come;
Achitophell so counsell'd Absalome."

B. ii. st. 2.

(The original has merely,—

" Ed or dalle spelonche, ove lontano
Dal vulgo esercitar suol l' arti ignote,
Vien," &c.)

Act iv. sc. 1.

" *Enter* HECATE *and the other three Witches.*"

When, in my *Remarks on Collier's and Knight's editions of Shakespeare,* p. 200, I said that " the other three Witches" are " *the three* who now enter for the first time, there being already *three* on the stage: the number of Witches in this scene is six,"—I made a great mistake, which was obligingly pointed out to me by Mr. Macready.

" *The other three Witches*" means the three already on the stage,—they being the *other* three, when enumerated along with Hecate, who may be considered as the chief Witch. *Three* Witches are quite sufficient for the business of the scene ; and, as far as concerns the effect to be produced on the spectators, are even more impressive than six.

Act v. sc. 3.

" And, with some sweet oblivious antidote,
Cleanse the *stuff'd* bosom of that perilous *stuff*
Which weighs upon the heart."

" From the writer of the manuscript notes in the folio, 1632, we learn that *grief* ought to have been inserted instead of 'stuff'." Collier's *Notes and Emendations*, &c. p. 416.

I must not be understood as positively maintaining the integrity of the old text, when I express my strong suspicion that the Manuscript-corrector altered "*stuff*" to "grief" merely because he was offended by an iteration which had gone much out of fashion at the time he wrote. Malone (in a note on the line) has already brought forward several* examples of similar repetitions from other plays of Shakespeare—(repetitions which, as well as his quibblings in serious dialogues, &c., the great poet would doubtless have avoided, had he lived in an age of severer taste); and I subjoin a variety of passages which will evince the fondness of our early authors for a jingle of that description;

"I *Harold* then, a *harauld* [*i. e.* herald] sent in haste."
King Harold,—*A Mir. for Magistrates*, &c. p. 248, ed. 1610.

"In *dreadfull* feare amid the *dreadfull* place."
Sackville's *Induction*,—*Id.* p. 261.

"Of which the kings *charge* doth me cleere *discharge*."
Tiptoft Earle of Worcester,—*Id.* p. 369.

"I saw the *polles* cut off from *polling* theeues."
Richard Neuill Earle of Warwicke,—*Id.* p. 374.

"My selfe heere *present* do *present* to thee
My life," &c.   The Lord Hastings,—*Id.* p. 411.

"On her [*i. e.* the Church] a strong hand violently laid,
Preying on that they gaue for to be *prai'd.*"
The Lord Cromwell (by Drayton),—*Id.* p. 539.

---

* Many more might be adduced,—such as,
"*Dy'd* in the *dying* slaughter of their foes."
King John, act ii. sc. 2.

"They *wreake* their vengeaunce in his *reeking* blood."
                King *Edward the Second*,—*Id.* (Contin. by
                        Niccols), p. 709.

"The cannons thicke discharg'd on either hand,
Wrapt *clouds* in *clouds* of smoake," &c.
                England's Eliza (by Niccols, appended to
                        A Mir. for Mag.), p. 828.

"For Hell and Darkness *pitch* their *pitchy* tents."
                Marlowe's *Tamburlaine, Sec. Part,—Works,*
                        i. 215, ed. Dyce.

"Whose *yielding* heart may *yield* thee more relief."
                Marlowe's *Dido,—Id.* ii. 413.

"Lyke as a trembling *hart,* whose *hart* is pierst with an
    arrow," &c.
                A. Fraunce's *Countess of Pembrokes Yuychurch,*
                        Part. Sec., 1591, sig. I 4.

"There was a *maide* soe *made* as men might thinck her a
    goddesse."
                Translation from Heliodorus,—appended to
                        the same, sig. M.

"O Duke of *Sore,* what great *sore* didst thou find,
To see thy noble sonne so foule betraid," &c.
                Harington's *Orlando Furioso,* b. xxxvi. st. 7.

"With true measur'd crowing the timely houres to speake,
And still against his *windie* sire to *winde* his beake."
                A Herrings Tayle, &c. 1598, sig. B 2.

"And not one *foot* his stedfast *foot* was moued," &c.
                Fairfax's *Tasso,* b. v. st. 63
(one of the innumerable things in that translation which are not
to be found in the original).

"Her garment *side* [*i. e.* long], and, by her *side*, her glaue."
Id. b. ix. st. 8.

"Were for the glorious *sunne*-shine of my *sonnes.*"
B. Barnes's *Diuels Charter*, 1607, sig. B 2.

"Whilst by my *furie Furies furious* made," &c.
W. Alexander's [Lord Stirling's] *Tragedie of Julius Cæsar*, sig. Q 4, ed. 1607.

"Great *Pompey's pomp* is past, his glorie gone."
Id. sig. R 2.

"And *force* his *forces* from the Brittish shores."
Armin's *Valient Welshman*, sig. C 3, ed. 1615.

"T' *inflame* the *Flamine* [*Flamen*] of Jove Ammon so," &c.
Sylvester's *Du Bartas*,—*First Day of the First Week*, p. 6, ed. 1641.

"And toward the *bottom* of this *bottom* [*i. e.* ball] bound."
Id.,—*Third Day of the First Week*, p. 25.

"Fair *rose* this *Rose* with truth's new-springing raies."
Id.,—*ibid.* p. 26.

"And *still*-green laurel shall be *still* thy lot."
Id.,—*ibid.* p. 29.

"Here, on a green, two *striplings stripped* light," &c.
Id.,—*Seventh Day of the First Week*, p. 59.

"There th' ugly *Bear bears* (to his high renown)
Seav'n shining stars."
Id.,—*The Columnes*, p. 141 [139].

"Where up he *mounts*, and doth their *Mount* surprise."
Id.,—*The Vocation*, p. 152.

"As black as *jet* they *jet* about." *Id.*,—*ibid.* p. 155.

"To *grave* this short remembrance on my *grave.*"
Drummond,—*Sonnet to Sir W. Alexander*
(a sonnet of great beauty, most carefully composed).

> " And, Reading [the name of the person addressed], of the
> world thou *read'st* aright."
>
> Hubert's *Edward the Second*, p. 129, ed. 1629.
>
> " There hang a gauntlet bright, here a stabt buckler,
> *Pile* up long *piles* [*i. e* darts]," &c.
>
> *Fuimus Troes*, 1633, sig.F 3.

I could easily adduce many other passages: but, not to weary the reader, I close the list with proofs that even the lofty Muse of Milton did not disdain a jingle;

> " That brought into this *world* a *world* of woe."
>
> *Par. Lost*, b. ix. 11.
>
> " He all their ammunition
> And *feats* of war *defeats*."
>
> *Samson Agon.* 1277.*

Further,—it may be asked if the Manuscript-corrector's alteration does not introduce a great impropriety of expression,—" CLEANSE the bosom of GRIEF"?

Act v. sc. 5.

> " And all our yesterdays have lighted fools
> The way to *dusty death*."

The commentators (who hunt for something parallel in the *Psalms,* Sidney's *Arcadia,* and *Pierce Plowman*) evi-

---

* The old Italian poets occasionally affect the same sort of repetition; *e. g.;*

> " Cosi, quando quell' altro hebb' egli scorto,
> Seco s' affronta, e in men ch' io non fauello,
> Hebbe il franco Rugger quel *Morte morto,*
> Che non potea trouar maggior flagello."
>
> Dolce,—*Prime Imprese del Conte Orlando,*
> c. xvii. p. 142, ed. 1572.

dently suppose that the very striking expression, "*dusty death*," is found for the first time in *Macbeth*. But I meet with it in a poem which was published more than a dozen years before the appearance of that tragedy;

> " Time and thy graue did first salute thy nature,
>   Euen in her infancie and cradle-rightes,
>   Inuiting it to *dustie deaths* defeature,
>   And therewithall thy Fortunes fierce despights:
>   Death is the gulfe of all: and then I say,
>   Thou art as good as Cæsar in his clay."
>   *A Fig for Fortune*, 1596, by Anthony Copley,
>   p. 57 [49].

HAMLET.

Act i. sc. 1.

"We may presume that in this first scene a cock was heard to crow, in order to give the Ghost notice of the fit time for his departure, *Cock crows* being placed in the margin opposite the words 'Stop it, Marcellus.'" Collier's *Notes and Emendations*, &c. p. 418.

The *cock* used *to crow* when Garrick acted Hamlet, and perhaps also when that part was played by some of his successors; but now-a-days managers have done wisely in striking out the *cock* from the list of Dramatis Personæ.

Act i. sc. 2.

"discourse *of* reason."

Boswell, by several examples, has supported the phraseology of the text against Gifford, who rather hastily asserted that we ought to read "discourse *and* reason." To the passages cited in Boswell's note, add the following one; "There was no *discourse of reason* strong enough to diuert him from thinking that he was betrayed." *A Tragi-comicall History of our Times, under the borrowed names of Lisander and Calista* (from the French), 1627, p. 34.

Act i. sc. 2.

"In my *mind's eye*."

So the Italians:—

> "E ch' io punisca il traditor di Gano
> D' un tradimento già, ch' io veggo scorto
> Con *gli occhi de la mente* in uno specchio," &c.
> Pulci,—*Morg. Mag.* c. xxiv. st. 4.

> "Ora a *l' occhio mentale* è conceduto
> Di riveder ciò che tu hai veduto."
> *Id.,—ibid.* c. xxv. st. 308.

Act i. sc. 2.
> " whilst they, *distill'd*
> Almost to jelly with the act of fear,
> Stand dumb, and speak not to him."

The quartos have "*distill'd;*" the folio has "*bestil'd.*" " Neither word, 'distill'd' or *bestill'd,* can be perfectly satisfactory; but it is apparent that *bestill'd* was a misprint in the folio, 1623 (and from thence copied into the folio, 1632), for a word, very like it in letters, but affording a very clear and sensible meaning:—

> 'Whilst they, *bechill'd*
> Almost to jelly with the act of fear,' &c.

Bernardo and Marcellus were almost chilled to jelly by their apprehensions, 'the cold fit of fear' having come powerfully upon them. This must be deemed a text superior to that of any old or modern edition." Collier's *Notes and Emendations,* &c. p. 420.

Is there not something strange in such an expression as "*human bodies* CHILLED *almost to* JELLY *by fear*"?

(One modern editor of Hamlet has given "bestill'd:" but I doubt if the verb *still* (to fall in drops, melt) ever was, or could be, used with the augmentative prefix *be*.)

Why should the "*distill'd*" of the quartos be considered as "not perfectly satisfactory?"—"they, *melted, dissolved* almost to jelly with the act of fear," &c. Examples of the word in that sense are not wanting in modern writers: a passage of Claudian (*De Sexto Cons. Hon.* v. 345),

"liquefactaque fulgure cuspis
Canduit, et subitis fluxere vaporibus enses,"—

is thus rendered by Addison,

"Swords by the lightning's subtle force *distill'd*,
And the cold sheath with running metal fill'd."
Remarks on Several Parts of Italy, &c. p. 208, ed. 1745.

Act i. sc. 4.

"*Ham.* The king doth wake to-night, and takes his *rouse*," &c.

Whatever may have been the original meaning of "*rouse*," and whatever may be its precise signification in the above line (see a long note on the word by Gifford—Massinger's *Works*, i. 239, ed. 1813), it undoubtedly was sometimes used in the sense of *a large draught of liquor;*

"Where slightly passing by the Thespian spring,
Many long after did but onely sup;
Nature then fruitfully forth these men did bring,
To fetch deepe *rowses* from Joues plenteous cup."
Drayton's Verses prefixed to Chapman's
Hesiod, 1618.

(Concerning "wake" in the present passage, see my *Remarks on Collier's and Knight's eds. of Shakespeare*, p. 210.)

Act i. sc. 4.
"why the sepulchre,
Wherein we saw thee quietly *in-urn'd*,
Hath op'd his ponderous and marble jaws,
To cast thee up again ?"

Perhaps the reading of the quartos (of *all* the quartos), "interr'd," is preferable, because "*in-urn'd*" implies that the body had been reduced to ashes. (Compare act i. sc. 1;

"What art thou, that usurp'st this time of night
Together with that fair and warlike form
In which the majesty of *buried* Denmark
Did sometimes march ?")

Act i. sc. 4.
"Which might *deprive* your sovereignty of reason."

There seems to be no doubt that Gifford was wrong in supposing "*sovereignty*" to be here "a title of respect;" and that the meaning is—Which might take away the sovereignty of your reason (or, as Steevens explains it, "take away from you the command of reason, by which man is governed").

In a note on Beaumont and Fletcher, *Works*, ix. 272, I have shewn that "*deprive*" is used there, as it is here, in the sense of—take away. Compare also;

s

> "And now, this hand, that, with vngentle force
> *Depryu'd* his life, shall with repentant seruice
> Make treble satisfaction to his soule."
>
> *The Tryall of Cheualry*, 1605, sig. F 3.

> "For pitty, do not my heart blood *deprive*,
> Make me not childless," &c.
>
> Sylvester's *Du Bartas*,—*The Magnificence*,
> p. 210, ed. 1641,

(where the original has "Ne me *priue du sang*," &c.).

> "But yet the sharp disease (which doth his health *deprive*)
> With-holdeth in some sort his senses and his wit," &c.
>
> *A Paradox against Liberty*, from the French of
> Odet de la Noue,—*ibid.* p. 313.

> "In short, this day our scepter had *depriv'd*,
> Had I not," &c.
>
> *The History of Judith*, translated by Hudson,—
> *ibid.* p. 377.

Act i. sc. 5.

> "Thus was I, sleeping, by a brother's hand,
> Of life, of crown, of queen, at once *despatch'd*."

"An advantageous proposal is made in the corrected folio, 1632 . . . . 'Dispatch'd' cannot be right, and why should Shakespeare employ a wrong word when another, that is unobjectionable, at once presented itself, viz.—

> 'Of life, of crown, of queen, at once *despoil'd*'?

Misreading was, most likely, the cause of this blunder; the earliest quarto, 1603, has *depriv'd* for 'dispatch'd,' of the other quartos and folios; but we may feel confident that the poet's misprinted word was *despoil'd*. It is written upon an erasure, and possibly the old corrector first inserted *depriv'd*, and afterwards saw reason to change it to *despoil'd*, as the true language of the poet." Collier's *Notes and Emendations*, &c. p. 422.

Why "despatch'd," the reading of all the old editions (for the quarto of 1603 is not of any authority), should be condemned by Mr. Collier as a decided error of the press, I am at a loss to conceive. The "proposal" of the Manuscript-corrector is so far from being "advantageous," that, strictly speaking, we lose something by it,—"*despoil'd*" conveying merely the idea of *deprivation*, while "despatch'd" expresses the *suddenness of the bereavement*.

Act i. sc. 5.

" The glow-worm shows the matin to be near,
And 'gins to pale his *uneffectual* fire."

According to Warburton, "*uneffectual*" means "shining without heat;" according to Steevens, "that is no longer seen when the light of morning approaches." The former explanation is, I apprehend, the true one. Compare Nash; "The moral of the whole is this, that as the Estrich, the most *burning-sighted* bird of all others, insomuch as the female of them hatcheth not hir egs by couering them, but by the *effectual raies* of hir eies," &c. *The Vnfortvnate Traveller. Or, The Life of Jacke Wilton*, 1594, sig. H 4.

Act ii. sc. 2.

" for his picture *in little*."

Here Steevens cites Rowley, Drayton, and Massinger. He might have shewn that the expression "*in little*" was used by writers long after the time of Shakespeare: so in Shadwell's *Sullen Lovers;* "I will paint with Lilly [Lely], and draw *in little* with Cooper for 5000*l.*" *Works*, i. 27.

Act ii. sc. 2.

"for it cannot be
But I am pigeon-liver'd and lack gall
To make *oppression* bitter; or, ere this,
I should have fatted all the region kites
With this slave's offal."

Mr. Collier observes; "It was not 'oppression,' but crime, that was to be punished by him; and to read [with the Manuscript-corrector of the folio]

'To make *transgression* bitter'

is so far an improvement: the similarity in the sound of the terminations of both words may have misled the copyist. 'Oppression' is, however, quite intelligible." *Notes and Emendations*, &c. p. 424.

This alteration is nothing less than villanous. Could the Manuscript-corrector be so obtuse as not to perceive that "lack gall to make *oppression* bitter," means "lack gall to make me feel the bitterness of oppression?"

Act iii. sc. 2.

"*Ham.* Ay, sir, but, *While the grass grows,*—the proverb is something musty."

Malone quotes this proverb in full from Whetstone's *Promos and Cassandra*, 1578,—

" *Whylst grass doth growe*, oft sterves the seely steede;"

and from *The Paradise of Daintie Devises*, 1578,—

" *While grasse doth growe*, the silly horse he starves."

I find it, with a variation, in Whitney's *Emblemes*, 1586;

" *While grasse doth growe*, the courser faire doth sterue."
p. 26.

Act iii. sc. 2.
" Now could I drink hot blood,
And do such business as the *bitter* day
Would quake to look on."

So Malone, adhering to the quartos; while Mr. Collier and Mr. Knight adopt the reading of the folios,—

" And do such *bitter* business as the day," &c.

All this is marvellous! Can any thing be plainer than that, in the quartos, " *bitter*" is a misprint for " better" (as it often is; *e.g.*;

" Here comes my *bitter* Genius, whose advice," &c.
A pleasant conceited Comedy, how to choose a good Wife from a bad, 1634, sig. G 4);

that the editor or printer of the folio, not perceiving that it was a misprint, made his stupid transposition; and that the genuine lection is,

" And do such business as the *better* day
Would quake to look on" ?

Did the modern editors never read in Milton,

"Hail, *holy Light*, offspring of Heaven," &c.?

Act iii. sc. 3.

"O, my offence is rank, it *smells to heaven!*"

So Petrarch;

"Or vivi sì che a Dio ne venga il lezzo."
Sonetto civ.

And see also Ariosto, *Orlando Furioso*, c. xviii. st. 23.

Act iii. sc. 4.

"A *station* like the herald Mercury," &c.

To shew that "station" means here *the act of standing* [or *manner of standing, attitude*], Theobald and Steevens quote our author's *Antony and Cleopatra*, act iii. sc. 3.— Other writers have employed the word in the same sense: so Fletcher;

"What a strange scene of sorrow is express'd
In different postures, in their looks and *station!*
A common painter, eyeing these, to help
His dull invention, might draw to the life," &c.
Lovers' Progress, act iv. sc. 3.

Act iii. sc. 4.

"Your bedded hair, like life in *excrements*,
Starts up, and stands on end."

In the *Variorum Shakespeare*, on the word "*excrements*," there is a note by Whalley, which is more to the purpose than much of the annotation in that *omnium gatherum:* still it may not be useless to cite here a passage from Chapman's *Justification of a strange action of Nero*, &c., 1629; " And albeit hayre were of it selfe the most abiect *excrement* that were, yet should Poppæas hayre be reputed honourable. I am not ignorant that hayre is noted by many as an *excrement,* a fleeting commodity . . . . . An *excrement* it is, I deny not," &c. Sig. B 2.

Act iii. sc. 4.

" His form and cause conjoin'd, preaching to stones
   Would make them *capable.*"

For examples of the word "*capable*," Malone, it would seem, was obliged to confine himself to the works of Shakespeare. Compare *Euerie Woman in her Humor*, 1609;

"*Ser.* We voide of hostile armes—
Hostis. I, if they had had horses, they had sau'd their armes.
Ser. Be capable [*i. e.* be intelligent,—understand me]. I meane, voide of armorie." Sig. D 4.

Act v. sc. 1.

" *A pick-axe, and a spade, a spade,*
   For—and *a shrouding sheet,*" &c.

In my *Remarks on Collier's and Knight's eds. of Shakespeare,* p. 218, I adduced several passages to prove that

the modern editors were wrong in putting a break after
"For." I subjoin another;

> "The boyle was vp, we had good lucke,
> In frost *for and* in snow."
>> Canting Song in Dekker's *English Villanies*, &c.
>> sig. o 2, ed. 1632.

Act v. sc. 1..

"*Imperious* Cæsar, dead, and turn'd to clay," &c.

So the quartos. The folio, "imperial;" which Mr. Collier and Mr. Knight adopt. Malone observes; "The editor of the folio substituted *imperial*, not knowing that *imperious* was used in the same sense. . . There are other instances in the folio of a familiar term being substituted in the room of a more ancient word."

The right reading, whether the passage be or be not a quotation (see Collier's *Notes and Emendations*, &c. p. 430), is, in all probability, "*imperious;*" which in Shakespeare's time was the usual form of the word. So in the Countess of Pembroke's *Tragedie of Antonie* (translated from the French), 1595,—

> "The scepters promis'd of *imperious* Rome."
>> Sig. G 3.

Even in Fletcher's *Prophetess*, written long after *Hamlet*, we have,—

> "'tis *imperious* Rome,
> Rome, the great mistress of the conquer'd world."
>> Act ii. sc. 3.

Act v. sc. 1.

"Anon, as patient as the female dove
When that her golden couplets are *disclos'd*," &c.

Disclos'd means—hatched. But I only notice the passage for the sake of pointing out to those who are curious in poetical phraseology the strange use of this word by Waller. In some lines *To the Queen-mother of France upon her Landing*, he addresses her as if she had been a second Leda;

" Great Queen of Europe! where thy offspring wears
All the chief crowns; where princes are thy heirs;
As welcome thou to sea-girt Britain's shore,
As erst Latona, who fair Cynthia bore,
To Delos was: here shines a nymph as bright,
By thee *disclos'd*, with like increase of light."

KING LEAR.

Act iii. sc. 4.

"Edg. *Child Rowland to the dark tower came,*
His word was still—Fie, foh, and fum,
I smell the blood of a British man."

Of the ballad here cited (and probably with some variation from the original) fragments of a Scottish version have been preserved by Jamieson in *Illustr. of Northern Antiquities,* &c. 4to, 1814. He gives (p. 402);

" With fi, fi, fo, and fum !
I smell the blood of a Christian man!
Be he dead, be he living, wi' my brand
I'll clash his harns frae his harn-pan,"

(*i. e.* I'll knock his brains out of his skull). Child Rowland, it appears, was the youngest son of King Arthur.

OTHELLO.

Act i. sc. 3.

"I therefore beg it not,
To please the palate of my appetite;
Nor to comply with heat, the young affects
In my defunct and proper satisfaction;
But to be free and bounteous to her mind:
And heaven defend your good souls, that you think
I will your serious and great business scant,
When [*Qtos* For] she is with me. No, when light-wing'd toys
Of feather'd Cupid seel [*Qtos* foil] with wanton dulness
My speculative and offic'd instrument [*Qtos* active instruments]," &c.

"We subjoin," says Mr. Collier, "the representation of the text as made by the corrector of the folio, 1632:—

'I therefore beg it not,
To please the palate of my appetite,
Nor to comply wi' the *young effects of heat*
(In *me* defunct) and proper satisfaction,
But to be free and bounteous to her mind:
And heaven defend your *counsels*, that you think
I will your serious and great business scant
When she is with me. No; when light-wing'd toys
Of feather'd Cupid *foil* with wanton dulness
My speculative and offic'd *instruments*,' &c.

In the third line it seems that 'heat' got transposed, while *of* was omitted; in the fourth line, *me* was misprinted 'my;' and in the sixth line, *counsels* became 'good souls,' terms Othello would hardly apply to the Duke and Senators of Venice. *Foil*, in the ninth line, agrees with the quartos, where *instruments* is also in the plural." *Notes and Emendations*, &c. p. 451.

One cannot but regret to see Mr. Collier labouring to account for an imaginary error in the old copies,—" 'heat' got transposed, while *of* was omitted." The error lies wholly with the Manuscript-corrector, whose emendation,—

"Nor to comply wi' the *young effects of heat*,"

is not only very violent, but altogether objectionable. In the opening of this speech no alteration whatever is required, except that of a single letter,—the change of "*my*" to "*me*" (which was made by Upton);

"Nor to comply with heat (the young affects
In *me* defunct) and proper satisfaction."

"*Affects*," says Johnson, (whose explanation is termed "rational and unforced" by Gifford, Massinger's *Works*, ii. 30, ed. 1813) "stands here not for *love*, but for *passions*, for that by which any thing is affected. *I ask it not*, says he, *to please appetite, or satisfy loose desires*, the passions of youth which I have now outlived, or 'for any particular gratification of myself,' but merely that I may indulge the wishes of my wife."—"*Young affects*" (writes Gifford, *ubi supra*) are therefore perfectly synonymous with *youthful heats*. Othello was not an old man, though he had lost the fire of youth; the critics might therefore have dismissed that concern for the lady, which they have so delicately communicated for the edification of the rising generation."

With respect to the other emendation of the Manuscript-corrector, "*counsels*" for "good souls," I would advise an editor of Shakespeare to weigh it well before he adopts it. What is the meaning of "Heaven *defend* your *counsels*"? (If "defend" be equivalent here, as Steevens supposes, to *forbid,* the alteration must be decidedly wrong.)

Act iii. sc. 3.

" I'd *whistle her off,* and let her down the wind," &c.

" *Ajetter un oiseau.* To cast, or *whistle off,* a hawke ; to let her goe, let her flie." Cotgrave's *Dict.*

Act v. sc. 1.

" *Iago.* Villainous *whore!*
 Emil. She gave it Cassio! no alas! I found it,
And I did give 't my husband.
 Iago. *Filth,* thou liest."

Here, when Iago calls his wife "*filth,*" he uses a term synonymous with the word he has just applied to her. Compare Greene's *Notable Discouery of Coosnage,* &c. 1592; " To him will some common *filth* (that neuer knew loue) faine an ardent and honest affection." Sig. c 4.

ANTONY AND CLEOPATRA.

Act i. sc. 2.

"I must from this enchanting queen break off;
Ten thousand harms, more than the ills I know,
My idleness doth hatch.—*How now!* Enobarbus!

Enter ENOBARBUS.
Eno. What's your pleasure, sir?"

So all editions,—with a flagrant error.

It would be impossible, I presume, to point out, in any old writer, an instance of "How now!" used as *the exclamation of a person summoning another into his presence.* Here the right reading is indubitably,—

"*Ho*, Enobarbus!"

I have already shewn* that "*ho*" was very frequently spelt "*how:*" and the probability is, that in the present passage the author's manuscript had "*how;*" to which either some transcriber or the original compositor, who did not understand what was meant, added "now" (making the line over-measure).

Act i. sc. 5.

"So he nodded,
And soberly did mount an *arm-gaunt* steed,

* See p. 56.

Who neigh'd so high, that what I would have spoke
Was *beastly* dumbe [dumb'd] by him."

" The first difficulty has arisen out of the epithet 'arm-gaunt,' and, without noticing other proposed emendations, we may state that Sir Thomas Hanmer's 'arm-*girt*' is precisely that of the old corrector, who also makes a very important change in the last hemistich, which, in the folios, stands,—

' Was beastly dumbe by him.'

The commentators have properly taken ' dumbe' as a misprint for *dumb'd*, and have referred to ' Pericles,' where *dumbs* is used as a verb. It seems that ' beastly' was not Shakespeare's word, which we can well suppose: in ' Macbeth' we have seen ' boast' misprinted *beast*, and in Henry V. (Chorus to Act iv.) we meet with the line,—

' Steed threatens steed in high and boastful neighs.'

In the passage before us, Alexas says that the 'arm-girt steed' neighed so 'high' that he could not address Antony: in what way, then, does the corrector of the folio, 1632, give the whole passage ?—

' So he nodded,
And soberly did mount an arm-*girt* steed,
Who neigh'd so high, that what I would have spoke
Was *boastfully* dumb'd by him.'

One slight objection to this change is that *boastfully* must be read as a dissyllable." Collier's *Notes and Emendations,* &c. p. 467.

" Arm-gaunt" has been variously explained,—*lean-shouldered, as thin as one's arm,* &c.: but Warburton's interpretation, *worn lean and thin by much service in war*, is the only one which would suit the passage; for, as Nares well observes (*Gloss*. sub v.), "all the rest of the senses are reproachful, and are therefore inconsistent with the speech which is made to display the gallantry of a lover to his mistress." Still, the interpretation of Warburton is at best extremely forced: and I make not the slightest doubt that the Manuscript-corrector and Sir Thomas Hanmer were right in considering "arm-gaunt" a misprint for "arm-*girt*."

But why did the Manuscript-corrector alter "beastly" to "*boastfully*" (which I should have thought nobody *could* "read as a dissyllable," had not Mr. Collier declared that it "*must* be read" as such)? Merely because he happened not to perceive the meaning which Shakespeare evidently intended "beastly" to convey, viz. *in the manner of a beast,* —i. e. *by inarticulate sounds*, which rendered vain all attempts at speaking on the part of Alexas. (The adverb "*beastly*" occurs in *The Taming of the Shrew*, act iv. sc. 2,

"Fie on her! see, how *beastly* she doth court him!"

and in *Cymbeline*, act v. sc. 3,

"and will give you that
Like beasts, which you shun *beastly*.")

Act ii. sc. 7.
"*Strike* the vessels, ho!
Here is to Cæsar."

"Strike" (which the commentators had strangely misunderstood) was first rightly explained by Weber, who shewed, from a passage in Fletcher's *Monsieur Thomas*, that it meant *tap*. Compare also *Love's Pilgrimage*, act ii. sc. 4 (by the same poet); " *Strike* me the oldest sack."

Act iii. sc. 4.

" When the best hint was given him, he not *took't*,
Or did it from his teeth."

Thirlby's emendation (first inserted in the text by Theobald).

" The folio, 1623, has 'he not look'd,' and the folio, 1632, 'he *had* look'd.' There appears no sufficient ground for doing more than amend the frequent error of 'not' for '*but;*' it avoids an awkwardness when Antony complains of Cæsar, that,—

' When the best hint was given him, he *but* look'd,
Or did it from his teeth.'

Such is the emendation in the folio, 1632, the meaning being, that Cæsar only look'd when the best hint was given him, or merely applauded Antony from his teeth, and not from his heart." Collier's *Notes and Emendations*, &c. p. 472.

The reading of the Manuscript-corrector has not only great obscurity of expression (Mr. Collier's explanation that " he but look'd" means " *he only look'd*," being rather an unsatisfactory one), but is also unsuited to what immediately follows,—

" he but look'd,
Or did it from his teeth."

I have little doubt that Thirlby's much simpler emendation, "*took't*" for "look'd" (*which alters only a single letter,—the first folio having* "look't") restores the genuine reading.

CYMBELINE.

Act ii. sc. 2.
"and this will witness outwardly,
As strongly as the *conscience* does within,
To the madding of her lord."

It may not be useless to observe that "*conscience*" is used here for *consciousness*. ("As strongly as his inward consciousness.")

Act iii. sc. 3.
" O, this life
Is nobler, than attending for a check;
Richer, than doing nothing for a *babe;*
Prouder, than rustling in unpaid-for silk."

" The old copies give the third line,—

'Richer than doing nothing for a *babe*,'

and Hanmer substituted ' bribe,' though bribes are seldom given for doing nothing, while Warburton has *bauble*, and Malone adhered to *babe*. All three are unquestionably wrong: the second line supposes a courtier to dance attendance, and only to obtain 'a check,' or reproof, for his pains; and the third line follows up the same notion that he does nothing, yet is rewarded with a blow: Shakespeare repeatedly uses *bob* (the word in manuscript in the margin of the folio, 1632) in this way; and *babe*, then pronounced with the broad open *a*, was miswritten for it: therefore, the passage, properly printed, appears to be this:—

> 'O! this life
> Is nobler, than attending for a check,
> Richer than doing nothing for a *bob*,' &c."
>
> Collier's *Notes and Emendations*, &c. p. 494.

Though Mr. Collier patronises this correction, I cannot help regarding it as singularly infelicitous,—the word "bob" being almost ridiculously improper in the mouth of the present speaker, who is moralising very gravely. (Mr. Collier is mistaken in saying that "Shakespeare repeatedly uses *bob*:" it is found but once throughout his dramas, viz. in *As you like it*, act ii. sc. 7,—" senseless of the *bob*.")

As to Malone's notion that "babe" could here signify puppet,—one can only wonder at it. Neither "*bauble*" (which is Rowe's, not Warburton's, emendation), nor "*bribe*" seem to suit the passage. In all probability, the right reading is "*brabe*." In a note ad l. Boswell observes; "*Heth* is thus explained by Speght in his Glossary to Chaucer: '*Brabes* and such like.' *Hething*, for so Mr. Tyrwhitt gives the word, he interprets—*contempt*."

THE END.